FREE AND FAITHFUL

FREE AND FAITHFUL

AN AUTOBIOGRAPHY

My Life
in the
Catholic
Church

BERNARD HÄRING

LIGUORI/TRIUMPH
Liguori, Missouri

Published by Liguori/Triumph
An Imprint of Liguori Publications
Liguori, Missouri

This book is a translation from the German *Geborgen und frei: Mein Lebeno.*

Library of Congress Cataloging-in-Publication Data

Häring, Bernhard, 1912–
     [Glaubenserfahrung in den Fährnissen des Lebens. English]
     Free and faithful : my life in the Catholic Church / Bernard
Häring. — 1st ed.
          p.   cm.
     ISBN 0-7648-0184-8
     1. Häring, Bernhard, 1912–   —Biography. 2. Catholic Church—
Clergy—Biography. I. Title.
BX4705.H37A3   1997
241'.042'092—dc21   97–35603

Translation copyright 1998 by Liguori Publications
Printed in the United States of America
02 01 00 99 98   5 4 3 2 1
First Edition in English

CONTENTS

CONTENTS

CONTENTS

INTRODUCTION

For a long time, I have fought off the entreaties of some of my friends who wanted me to write an autobiography. What finally made me decide to try to record the story of my life was the gentle but emphatic urging of a friend who said, "Come on, an autobiography is not just about you. Don't you owe a debt to the Giver of all good gifts—and to us—to offer a testament of praise for God's ways of grace?"

So, dear reader, I have decided to offer you this interpretation of the story of my life as a story of faith. Perhaps, as you read and reflect on my life story, you will decide to interpret your own life in the light of *your* experience of faith. Perhaps you, too, will try to put your memories and thoughts in this perspective, and even write them down for yourself, for your friends, and for your heirs. I think especially of your heirs who, because you give them a chance to share your story of faith, will be your debtors for a particularly rich legacy. And, last but not least, this sort of enterprise will help you, as it did me, to maintain a grateful and fruitful memory.

My existence and the story of my life are closely connected to the faith story of many other men and women, but most particularly that of my parents, whose profound faith was a source of great joy to them.

The last time I visited my father, in 1947, we went on a long walk in the woods and discussed some of the important events of our lives. We shared a stirring litany. Then my father brought up a memory that was particularly precious to me: "Your life," he said, though not in these exact words, "is entirely woven around by the faith of your dear departed mother and around my own faith." And then he made an unforgettable point that gave me a great deal of happiness: "You and your eleven brothers and sisters were not born by accident. You were each a blessing from God, a gift from God that we prayed for and received with thanks. Every time before we had a child, both your mother and I prayed for that blessing. And during the nine months you were in your mother's womb, we often asked God's blessing for you.

"The day of your baptism was an especially great day of thanksgiving for us." Then he recalled another very significant and special memory. "You were born early on a Sunday morning," he recounted, "and you were baptized on the same day after high Mass. I was terribly disappointed because at the very hour of your baptism, I had to drive a very important gentleman home in my landau (carriage). We had just left the village behind us when the bells began to ring in honor of your baptism. The man asked me what the bells meant.

"My eleventh child," my father told him, "a boy named Bernard, is being baptized at this moment. It is rather hard for me that I cannot be there." The well-to-do gentleman started to say how sorry he felt for my father because of all the demands—financial and otherwise—that these many children would place on him, but my father gave him a powerful response. "There is no need to moan about it. Neither you nor anybody else has to pay for their daily bread and their education. My children are my wealth and my pride." Thank you, father, for telling me that before your death!

INTRODUCTION

So the story of my life and faith is based entirely on the blessing of my parents and of the people who helped them to ground our family so deeply in a joyful faith. I will now try to tell the story of my life against this backdrop, as an account of faith-experiences that blossomed amid the dangers of a life lived in a time of great and momentous events.

Bernhard Häring

FREE AND FAITHFUL

CHAPTER 1

FAMILY AND CHILDHOOD

I was born on November 10, 1912, in the village of Böttingen in southern Germany, the eleventh of twelve children, and heartily welcomed by the whole family. I cannot even imagine what a misfortune it must be for a child to sit at the kitchen table as an unwanted guest of the family.

Both my parents were deeply pious believers. My father came from a prosperous family: his father owned a brewery. He was also a landlord and a farmer. My father used to tell us that when he was a boy he often felt guilty eating his substantial sandwiches while the other children looked on, because he knew that their fathers had squandered the little money they had had on drink in *his* father's tavern. He swore that he would never be an innkeeper.

My mother, too, came from a family of farmers who were considered well-off back then. Her two older brothers had pressed her into taking over the estate, since they themselves did not feel they could pay out to all their brothers and sisters the share each had coming to them.

I spent my childhood as a farm boy in an utterly traditional mountain village. The power of that tradition and custom guaranteed a high degree of stability. You always knew where you stood and what was expected of you and everyone else.

In the village there was a class system that had never been challenged. There were the handful of "big farmers," though in today's terms, of course, they would be "small farmers." The criterion was how many horses you had. The upper class were simply called "horse farmers." Then came the "cow farmers" and, bringing up the rear, the "goat farmers." The few artisans we had in our village belonged to none of these three classes, but they enjoyed a special prestige. The pastor of the local church was simply called "milord," and the status of the teacher and the mayor followed a considerable distance behind. One new element in the formula was the harmonica factory. Despite the rigidities of the old scheme of things, the well-to-do realized that it was their obligation to take care of the poorest of the poor.

In spite of the fact that our village was small, some prospects of the world beyond impinged on us. Though our milieu was narrow, it had various windows on the outside world. From the summit of "High Mountain," one could see, on clear days, a splendid panorama of the Swiss Alps. Our family was often visited by relatives from villages over six miles away. Most adult males made their Easter duty in Beuron, which was about seven miles away. And, before he got married, my father had spent a year in Zurich with an uncle.

Parents As Partners in Faith

In our family, there was never a trace of patriarchy—nor of matriarchy either. We could see for ourselves what true partnership was. Both our parents were highly gifted and capable persons. One day, when my father was already an old man, and my mother had long since died, he said, "Your mother was always the living Gospel for me." And in fact that is what we found her to be. One example should suffice to make this point clear. My father was complaining about an accident in the barn. Mother gave him a loving look. When father failed to react to it, she said, "But, Johannes, where is your faith?" He calmed down at once.

I never saw my parents quarrel. When they disagreed about something, they dealt with it openly and politely. I was never punished by my father, though he sometimes chided me in a calm tone of voice. My older brothers told me that father had occasionally punished them severely, until one day mother told him, "Johannes, if there has to be punishment, then you had better leave it to me. Your hand is too harsh." Father steadfastly accepted the suggestion. Still, I remember that once he said to mother, "But surely *now* it is time to punish the children for their fighting!"

Our parents never shouted at us. If mother had to take us to task for something, she never finished without a word of encouragement. We took it as an "advance of trust" in us that we did not want to forfeit under any circumstances. On the basis of this experience, I like to translate the classic theological phrase "prevenient grace" as an "advance of trust from God." This point of view plays an important role in my approach to morality and my whole way of thinking, and it arose from my mother's kindly actions even when she was chastising us.

As far as I can recall, my mother very rarely spanked us, and even then only in a symbolic sort of way. It didn't hurt, because it was an expression of kindness. Virtually the only time she punished us was when we came to her with accusations against one another. As she amiably explained, "You will just have to learn to clean up your little quarrels yourselves." That was, so to speak, the foundation of my later ethics of peace and my basic concern for nonviolence.

Our parent's faith was the air we breathed. According to my great-aunt (the grandmother of the later Federal Chancellor Kurt Georg Kiesinger), even as a young man my father was a weekly communicant. During my childhood he went to Communion daily, often after he had already worked for several hours. My mother was no less devout, but of course housework and caring for us children did not allow her to attend daily Mass. She blessed each of us children with holy water in the morning and in the evening. My parents' devotion was a healthy one, without a breath of sentimental piety.

In my parents' house we never ate together without praying together. When the Angelus bell rang, three times a day, all working and talking came to a halt. From October to April, the whole family recited the rosary and the Litany of Loreto every evening, with mother leading the prayers. In wintertime, mother would then read from *The Golden Legend* or some other pious book that recounted the lives of the saints. Frequently, this reading was followed by a casual conversation about religion, conducted in my mother's spontaneous fashion. Thus we learned organically, as it were, to see the events of life in the light of faith.

THE SHADOWS OF WORLD WAR I

Not long before I turned three, long shadows were cast over my childhood by the First World War, which hit our family hard. My uncle Martin, who lived in our house and was unsurpassed in his fondness for children, had to report for duty as soon as the war broke out. The next year it was my eldest brother Heinrich's turn. Both spent years at the front, and, as a result, we were in constant fear for their lives. Their trips home on leave, never without a little present for the smaller children, are stamped in my memory. My brother Heinrich once heard me say, "I'm scared of you." Was the man in that strange uniform really my brother? His whole appearance, and all the fuss over it, made me nervous. I was a child confronting something that simply shouldn't have been allowed, and that discomfort, for me, saturated the whole atmosphere in the house.

I was around five years old when father and my second-oldest brother, Wenzel, had a loud and angry argument. Several months before he was old enough to be drafted, Wenzel had volunteered. Under the laws then in force, this was the only way to keep my father from having to serve in the war. On the one hand, my father vehemently insisted that it was dishonorable for him as a father to let himself be ransomed by his son. He said that he would not be able to take it emotionally if Wenzel were killed. For his part, Wenzel appealed to father's conscience. "Your little children need you. You can manage without me!"

A full year later, there was a no less tragic a conflict between father and Heinrich, who was home on leave. When the time of his leave was up, Heinrich explained to our parents, "The war is hopelessly lost. I won't put up with it anymore. I'll say good-bye to you where everyone can see me. Then at night I'll steal back and hide out until the war is over." We all heard the argument even though they spoke quietly. Finally, father told the local pastor about it; and the priest convinced Heinrich to return to the front. Scarcely had he gotten there than he wrote a letter of apology and mentioned that Wenzel's regiment was stationed very near his. They had already agreed to meet, but the meeting was destined not to take place.

On the same day, the postman arrived with missing-in-action reports for both of my brothers. He knew that my mother was seriously ill; and he figured there was a danger she might die if she got this grim message. So he handed both letters to a close relation of ours, a clever and sensitive woman, entrusting her with the job of passing on the news in the most considerate way possible. This she succeeded in doing—with my father. But how was my father to inform us gently? He called us all together and asked us to pray, even as he could no longer hold back his tears. He struggled for breath, until he finally managed to tell us the grim facts. Then he implored us not to enter mother's bedroom with eyes red from crying. "Otherwise," he warned, "she'll die, too." We all broke out crying, the two youngest, naturally, Rosa and myself, most of all. My older brothers and sisters pulled themselves together. When my older sisters had washed their faces, two of them visited mother. But she was clairvoyant and immediately asked, "Which of the two has fallen?" And when there was no answer, she was stunned and groaned, "So it was both of them?"

For days after that, my mother hovered between life and death. I suppose the only reason she survived the crisis was the strength of her faith and her love for us.

After a while, we got a letter from a Scottish soldier, who sent on to us Heinrich's last greetings and his identity card, along with the news that he had seen Heinrich die. After another long period of time, word came that Wenzel was in an English POW camp.

Another year passed, and Wenzel was released, and came home with ugly cancerous ulcers all over his neck. The local doctors declared the disease incurable. My father went with Wenzel to a cancer specialist in Tübingen, who prescribed a vegetarian diet and long fasts, which were to be repeated at least once every year. To everyone's amazement,

Wenzel recovered. He followed the doctor's orders to the letter. Although he suffered relapses, he lived to a ripe old age.

These are my most troubling memories from the First World War. So many other families had similarly painful experiences. They left a permanent mark on our minds, even as we wrestled with the problem of coming to terms with them in faith. Again and again the question arises, "So is not God helpless in the face of the madness of wars?" But God cannot be responsible for the headstrong decisions of human beings. Given our free will, we have to ask ourselves a radically different question. "What can we do with our common faith in the one God and Father of us all in order to overcome the insanity of war or avoid it altogether?"

LIFE IN A LARGE FAMILY

As two of the twelve Häring children had died in early childhood, after Heinrich's death there were still nine of us left. Life together and family cohesiveness taught us more than anything else. We loved one another and were not a little proud of one another.

The ones closest to me were Rosa, who was three years younger than I was, and Elizabeth and Agatha, who were two and four years older, respectively. Martin was six years older. He felt comfortable playing the role of advocate when the girls seemed to be getting the upper hand. Every now and then we did have conflicts, but there was never any resentment. My eldest sister, Maria Ursula, was relatively young when she married a carpenter from the area. She became the mother of nine children. One of her sons, Bernard, became a Redemptorist. Sadly, he died at the age of fifty.

Martin emigrated with Wenzel to Brazil, and from there to the United States, where he founded a family. Five of my sisters became nuns. They have done exemplary work in the care of the sick, in the area of education, and, above all, in the care of the handicapped.

Among all my brothers and sisters, I had an especially close relationship with Konstantine, who was ten years older than I, and likewise with Walburga, who was eight years older. My mother entrusted me to them. They were, as people used to say, "child maids." Konstantine, I felt, was most like my mother. In preparing me for my first confession and first holy Communion, my mother expressly entrusted me to Konstantine, though of course without abandoning her own indispensable maternal role.

All my life I felt I was on the same wavelength as Konstantine. On the day of my first Communion, she was the only one to whom I dared reveal my secret. "I think I want to be a saint," I admitted to her. Of course, I was intent on hearing what she would say to that. I would have thought it perfectly understandable if she had answered, "Then you'll have to behave a whole lot better." She said nothing of the sort. With loving encouragement, she said, "Well, why not?"

However, at first, the only person I told about my wish to become a missionary was my mother. It was after Christmas in 1923. One day when everyone else was out of the house, I pulled myself together and clearly spoke my mind. I realized that I wasn't a model boy, and so I sheepishly added: "But they call me Bernard, the rascal."

I was overflowing with *joie de vivre* and kept having crazy new adventures, of which I'll mention just one. My godmother and my uncle (my mother's brother) lived on a large farm about a mile and a quarter from our house. I often walked there all by myself. My uncle's family had as many children as ours, and I got along especially well with Hannes (Johannes Flad). Roaming free in the barnyard was a billy goat with powerful horns. As he grew stronger and stronger, so did I. I used to like to grab him by the horns when he came up to me. It was a friendly tussle to see which of us was the stronger. Finally, the goat became so accustomed to our little game that he anticipated my visits. So whenever the goat began to take on a combative pose by lowering his mighty horns that meant, "Bernard must be on the way."

DECISION FOR THE PRIESTHOOD

When I decided to study to be a missionary, my godmother said to Hannes, "If your friend Bernard, that troublemaker, has the nerve to study for the priesthood, why don't you try it too?" And, in fact, Hannes decided to go along with me to apply at the preparatory school for the seminary. In a trip that lasted two days, we traveled to Gars (a little Bavarian town forty miles or so east of Munich) on the River Inn, where the Redemptorists had a six-form secondary school called a *Progymnasium*.

We stopped in Ulm, where for the first time in our lives we saw tomatoes for sale. They were cheap, so we bought a pound. Back on the train, Hannes took his first bites, then threw them out the window in disgust. I, too, had my doubts as to whether such things were really edible.

In Gars, we took the entrance exam for the second form in the *Progymnasium*. In school, we found boys from all over southern Germany. But in Gars we were practically the only ones who spoke the Alemannic dialect. At first, we had to get used to the prevailing Old Bavarian dialect. We could understand Hochdeutsch, but we couldn't speak it fluently.

Hannes and I were pretty good in all subjects, but in Latin we were very weak. Up until then, we had taken a total of about ten hours worth of Latin lessons from our pastor.

But these lessons were sufficient to give us a chance. I flung myself into the subject and, on the first class exam, I got an *A*, while Hannes only got a *C*. Even so, I think that he was always the more diligent student of the two of us.

Back home, I had been more interested in horses and the barn than in school. I would never have devoted myself to my studies for the sake of knowledge. You could say that as a student I was lively but rather lazy. My sister, Elizabeth, who was two years older than me but who sat in the same room with me in our four-class school, announced to mother from time to time, "Bernard didn't do his homework again." Now that my newfound industriousness was winning me such success, more so than Hannes, I wondered *Why take so much trouble?* On my next assignment, I got a *B*, and Hannes got his usual *C*. On the last assignment, it was the other way around. Hannes got a *B*; I got a *C*. I didn't make any tragic scenes over it, but Father Schuster, our teacher, did. On my first report card from the *Progymnasium*, there was a *B* for effort, with the observation that "this highly gifted student could be far more attentive and diligent." By contrast, Hannes got an *A+* for effort. Father read me the riot act, though mother did not take it so seriously. They did not set Hannes before me as a model, and we went along together in constant friendship all the way to ordination.

AT THE ALPHONSIANUM

Since the *Progymnasium* went only so far, Hannes and I moved to the Alphonsianum, in Günzburg, a Bavarian town not far from Augsburg. Though we boarded at the Alphonsianum, we went to school at the public *Gymnasium*. Even there, Hannes was always well ahead of me in diligence, while my grades as a whole barely beat his across the finish line.

This state-run school was another new world, with students and teachers of different religious beliefs or none at all, and with classes made up of both girls and boys.

The only girl in our class was my strongest rival. No doubt Josefa worked harder than I did. We were friends with each other, but in quite an unsentimental fashion. She cordially awarded the palm to me when, at the end of the year, I finished first in my class and was allowed to give the ceremonial speech. Almost fifty years later, after the operation on my larynx, I was giving lectures at the Catholic Academy in Augsburg, a gray-haired woman came up to congratulate me. I thanked her amiably, only to hear her say, "Don't you recognize me? I am Josefa!"

IN THE NOVITIATE

After I got my "absolutorium," a university certificate attesting to the fact that I had taken the requisite number of terms of study, Hannes and I entered the closed milieu of the Redemptorist novitiate in Deggendorf on the Danube, on the edge of the Bavarian Forest.

At the time of my entrance into the novitiate, when my father brought me to the train station, he asked me: "Why are you going so far away? Could you not become a diocesan priest?" My answer basically was: "I do not feel like a hero. I need the support and encouragement of a community." This made a lot of sense to him. Nevertheless he added: "Whatever you decide is right with us. If you return to us, you are also welcome. And if you should again take up your earlier plan about studying medicine, we will be helpful in that as well."

Hannes and I took this step together in May 1933, a few months after Hitler had come to power. Once again we had said, "We will try it out together." After around three months, Hannes let me know: "I've made my decision. I am staying." I had made the same decision.

FIRST VOWS

In May 1934, I took my first vows as a Redemptorist in Gars on the River Inn. To this day, I am amazed that my superiors were willing to take such a risk with me then. In the novitiate, I had tried to become a saint, if that were possible, in one year. I followed all the advice of the experienced Master of Novices, as well as his directives for living consciously at all times in the presence of God. When I noticed that he disliked my doing gymnastic exercises in the monastery garden, I gave them up completely. But the lack of exercise and my severe, self-imposed discipline brought on a bad collapse. I was beset with heart troubles and continuous severe headaches. The house physician, Dr. Englert, did what he could for me but, after a while, he told the Master of Novices, "Send this sick fellow away. You can absolutely count on it. He will never be capable of work."

The Master of Novices told me this verdict with tears in his eyes. Nevertheless, he decided to consult a well-known woman diagnostician in Munich. She examined me and then gave me instructions, like a loving mother, to take up a healthy regimen of gymnastics and sports for diversion. With firm conviction, she told the Master of Novices: "No, don't send Bernard away. He has a strong constitution." My superiors gave me the advance of trust that I needed. I took my first vows, even though I had to do it sitting in a chair.

I then began my studies at the Redemptorist college, and I also diligently performed my limbering-up exercises. At that time, the third class in the afternoon was Church history. Father Englebert Zettl, who taught the course, was

also our superior. When we had our first monthly conference, I was expecting him to ask me why I almost always
slept for a quarter-hour in his class. Since he never raised the
issue with me, I asked him, "I sit right in front of your nose.
What are you thinking when you see me sleeping almost every day?" I will never forget his laconic answer. "What should
I think. I say to myself, 'I hope that nap is doing him good.'"
That understanding went further toward my recovery than
all the limbering-up exercises in the world.

Back then, in May 1934, our brothers caught two moth-
erless roebuck fawns. They were entrusted to my care, and I
raised them with baby bottles of milk. They were soon eating out of my hand. When they got bigger, they would always charge joyfully up to me whenever I came by. Every
morning when I arrived, they would wrestle with each other
and race to see who would get to me first. Then they stood
before me wheezing with the effort.

All this physical exercise and animal husbandry was no
meaningless diversionary maneuver. It was the play of inner
energies pressing me toward health; it was joy in life and
nature. Very soon, I no longer needed a doctor. I had discovered a healthy lifestyle—healthy, too, when it came to fostering piety.

ORDINATION

In May 1939, along with five fellow Redemptorists, Hannes
and I were ordained to the priesthood by Michael Von
Faulhaber, cardinal archbishop of Munich. Together we celebrated our first Mass at home in Böttingen. At that time,
they did not yet have concelebration. So Hannes first sang a
Gregorian-chant Mass; then I was the main celebrant at a
Mass with a many-voiced choir. As I said my first Mass, the

rain poured down outside. We two, Hannes and I, were op-
timists and read the weather to mean, "All blessings come
from on high." As the old German saying has it, *Es regnet,
Gott segnet*" ("It is raining, God blesses").

Our paths did not separate until the autumn of 1939,
when we were drafted. My friend Johannes Flad fell at the
siege of Leningrad, as he tried, despite a warning from his
commander, to rescue wounded men from the line of fire. A
few days before the announcement of his death, his beloved
parents received a letter from him in which he wrote, "If you
should soon receive the news that I have fallen, do not mourn!
We know why we have lived." Only God knows how much
I owe my friend Hannes. My sorrow is just how many splendid men like him were involuntary victims of the crazed deeds
of one individual, Adolf Hitler, but also of the failure of so
many people to share responsibility for peace and for the
common good!

Let one seemingly small episode serve as a reminder of
Hannes's fine character. During our years of study in Gars,
fuel was scarce. Hence, we were allowed to heat our rooms
only when two people moved in together. As a matter of
course we had been assigned to the same room, but Hannes
went off on his own. He said to me, "Two tough farm boys
like us can manage for a good long time without a heated
room." Shortly before Christmas—it was exam time—I visited Hannes in his room, which was next to the bathroom. I
saw that the water in his wash basin was frozen. I looked at
Hannes, expecting him to say now, "I guess it's time to move
in together." But he had no idea of doing any such thing. So
I said, "Hannes, I'm freezing." At once, he began preparing
to move into a shared room so that we could have the benefit
of heat.

CHAPTER 2

YEARS OF STUDY IN THE MONASTERY

B ack then the provincial study house of the Redemptorists was located in Rothenfeld, a beautiful spot between the Ammersee and the Starnbergersee, two large lakes southeast of Munich. As often as I could, I went swimming in the nearby lakes. I also liked to help out on our farm during harvesttime. Thus the study of philosophy and theology became localized, bound up with my joy in the beauty of nature.

Apart from the ethics course, I enjoyed all the subjects taught. As a student, I was interested but not overly diligent. Father Alois Guggenberger had arrived from Louvain as a newly minted philosopher. The way he blazed his own trail as a teacher of philosophy was refreshing and infectious. He liked to get involved in disputations, and I enjoyed contradicting him when his theses failed to convince me. Thus I experienced philosophy not as a closed system, but as a joyful quest, as a reaching out for an overview, as a way of knowing the limits of our insight and vision.

My Enthusiasm for Religious Sociology

Father Untergehrer taught us sociology with enormous enthusiasm, concentrating above all on social theory. He was extremely convincing, but no genius, but his enthusiasm was somehow contagious. Besides, in this area lay a focal point of my own interest.

In my last year in the *Gymnasium,* I had written a play attacking the stubbornness of the East Prussian Junkers. It was called *The Social Deed.* Its hero was a large landholder, whose conscience had opened his eyes. He thoughtfully takes counsel with his tenants and workers to find a way for all of them to be coowners of the land. In their earnest searching among members of their group, they discover new paths on which they can all agree. The social deed becomes infectious.

But (as the plot progresses) the hard-boiled Junkers band together. They insist that the landholder has become a traitor and has to return to the old order. But the landholder stands fast. He prophetically challenges his opponents to free themselves from the old, unjust system; whereupon they cruelly kill him. As they complete the deed, the murderers stare at one another in horror. Suddenly, the play ends with a messenger appearing on the scene with the disastrous news, "The Soviet Army has just taken Königsberg. The front line is right around the corner."

By a strange coincidence, near the end of my time on duty in World War II, my retreating unit found itself in exactly the place I had chosen for the backdrop of my student drama. The wagons of the refugees, most of them drawn by four horses, were thrust into the ditches by units of the fleeing German army. There were scenes of despair as both civilians and soldiers rushed for safety.

The reader can imagine from this example how questions of social justice have held me in their grip from the time of my early studies all the way into old age. I always considered these questions to be matters of survival, of epoch-making and worldwide urgency. Of course, neither we as students nor our professors could see the dimensions of the North-South conflict, which has become so important today. For us back then, the "rich North" was embodied in the stubborn large landowners, who fought off all social reforms.

THE INFLUENCE OF THE STUDY OF HISTORY

Father Englebert Zettl, a thoroughly likable, good-humored man, taught us Catholic Church history with great dedication. As far back as the days of my high-school education, I had been deeply interested in history; and all during those years, I had read a lot of history books on my own. Church history in the narrower sense kept prompting me to explore the history of the non-Christian religions. I was impressed by the way Father Zettl, without a trace of apologetics, introduced us to the real history of the Church. I still remember well how during his lecture on the Babylonian Captivity of the popes, one of our most gifted students fainted—presumably out of shock—and slid out of his chair onto the floor. To this day, I am grateful to Father Zettl for the way he showed us that the Church, in his words, "doesn't need any pious lies."

True love for the Church faces the checkered reality of its past, ending with a song of praise that, despite everything, Christendom lives on and bears witness in many ways to the Gospel. There was no mistaking the fact that the professor who confronted us so implacably with the darkest sides of the Church did it out of a love for the Church and a dedication to the cause of Christ that could not be doubted. He was very helpful to me.

MY FIRST BRUSH WITH THE STUDY OF ETHICS

From the third year on, we had a daily ethics class in the third period. I found it totally boring. Our professor, Father Schmid, had gotten a double doctorate both in canon and in civil law (*doctor utriusque legis*) in Rome—only to have to lecture on moral theology, a state of affairs that back then was unfortunately regarded as normal. Even though he wasn't teaching in his area of training, he was further handicapped by using a textbook written by Joseph Aertnys, C.Ss.R., and C. A. Damen, which treated morality in an incredibly legalistic fashion. My classroom neighbor, August Hartmann, and I practically vied with each other as sleepers, each of us dozing off for at least fifteen minutes during Father Schmid's lectures. When we suspected that Father Schmid had seen us, we made a note of it in the book and learned by heart the passages we had slept through. We guessed these very passages would come up on the exam. Despite our distaste for this way of teaching moral theology, the two of us always got the highest marks in the subject of moral theology—a tragedy.

But I didn't leave my study of moral theology at that stage. Browsing in our library, I discovered the tremendous systematic outlines of moral theology by the nineteenth-century German theologians Johann Michael Sailer and Johann Baptist Hirscher, and I eagerly studied them "for comparison." Fortunately, it was around that time that Fritz Tillmann published his multivolume work on morality as the imitation of Christ. I studied it from cover to cover. Now I could get a clearer picture of some alternatives to what I was getting in class. Perhaps it was providential for my later work that I had to experience the whole gamut of approaches. Of course, I had no way of knowing then that my superiors would choose me as Father Schmid's successor.

SCRIPTURAL STUDIES

For Old Testament studies, we had the highly learned Father Schaum-berger, who had trained at the Biblical Institute in Rome and who was expert in many ancient languages—Hebrew, Aramaic, and so on. Although his lectures were often disorganized, I found them absorbing. But I positively could not swallow what he taught us about the verbal inspiration of Scripture—a complete toeing of the Roman line. When I returned to Gars after the war and read the encyclical *Divino Afflante Spiritu* by Pope Pius XII (edited by the future Cardinal Augustin Bea), I asked my dear old colleague what he thought now about these issues. He then revealed to me the utter abyss of pain he had felt at having to teach this old-fashioned approach to the inspiration of Scriptures "out of obedience." This had cost him an immense inner effort.

Our professor for New Testament studies was Father Brandhuber, an erudite and skillful teacher. His lectures were a pleasure for me; I even enjoyed his tests. I also chose this pious and learned man as my confessor. Finally, he was one of the professors who strongly urged my superiors to have me trained as a professor of moral theology. Later, when he was sick for a long time, I took my turn, as an old orderly, sitting up with him at night. Every few hours we had to change his shirt, which was completely soaked through with sweat. It was hard work, because the man was almost immobile. One night, when we had just finished this job, he waved me over. He had, he said, some good news, "Now I have finally understood it. I want to be dissolved and be with Christ." Then he added, "Now my unfinished manuscripts do not bother me anymore." From that moment he stopped sweating until the day he died, which wasn't long afterward. I owe a great deal to this man, my teacher and my friend.

Our professor of dogmatic theology was Father Viktor Schurr, an outstanding scholar with a sharp eye for the signs of the time. Later I will note how Father Schurr shared my first experience of the mission to the German Catholic refugees. He was capable of both pointing out new paths and taking them himself. He also was very understanding when I spoke my mind about the state of moral theology in those days. Even back then, and still more later on when I was his colleague, his incredible familiarity with the latest publications and his willingness to share this information with me came in very handy. Further, he would always lend me the most useful books and was most willing to share them with me.

Voting Against the Nazis

During our studies in Rothenfeld, we lived through some dramatic events. At election time under Hitler, we had to vote in the town of Andechs. We were stupefied when we read in the newspaper after one such election that 100 percent of the voters had said yes to Hitler—this despite the fact that all of us had voted against him. At the next election, an order came from above that a special polling place would be opened in Rothenfeld "to spare us the walk to Andechs." Naturally, the only reason for this order was to keep our ballots under strict surveillance. After we had some heated discussions over this matter, and in the end, we all decided to publicly vote *No*. However, late in the evening before the election, our provincial superior arrived in a state of extreme concern. He made it clear to us that the reaction to our decision by higher-ups might be devastating. Some of us responded to this news with an extremely radical stance: our consciences were at stake; and, whether we liked it or not, *everything* was at stake here. After a long argument, we agreed that while we would not vote *No*, we would just hand in blank ballots, declaring that this was not a free election. All of us were aware of the tragic implications of what we were doing. The Nazis took no direct measures immediately, but they soon filed a suit over foreign exchange funds that ended with the confiscation of our theological college in Rothenfeld. Fortunately, we were able to move to Gars, though consolidation caused some crowding there.

Around that time we had students from Brazil in Rothenfeld and, at first, in Gars as well. Their presence also somehow offered protection against political pressures. I used the opportunity to get a good grasp of Brazilian Portuguese. The provincial superior still meant to send me, as I had requested, to Brazil once I had finished my studies.

FINALLY A REDEMPTORIST

After the final exam, which I passed with flying colors, at the humanistic Gymnasium in Günzburg, I had hesitated awhile about whether I should become a Redemptorist or a Jesuit. I was familiar with the Jesuits from their great missionaries in Asia. But I made inquiries and learned that they had a two-track program of studies, one for the more gifted, with a view to teaching, and a second aimed instead at pastoral care, including missionary work. I would have fallen into the first category, and that made entry to the Jesuits out of the question for me.

Before I made my formal request to be admitted to the Redemptorists, I expressly asked the provincial whether he could guarantee that I would be a missionary and not a professor. He said he could promise me that with about 90 percent certainty. After my ordination in Gars, in May 1939, I had a talk with the provincial (the same man I had met in

1933). He was completely in favor of my going to Brazil. But in the summer when it was time to buy the ticket for passage to Brazil by ship, he himself came to my room and told me that he had been sharply criticized by the professors at the seminary. So he had to accede to their wishes and send me on for further study to become a professor of moral theology.

I frankly told him that that was the last thing I wanted, that I had an insurmountable aversion to a legalistic moral theology. His answer was this: "That is exactly what the professors and I wanted; we expect that you will commit yourself to a fundamental renewal of the field of moral theology." Given this unequivocal advance of trust, I could only say yes. And, thus, an important decision had been reached. But rather soon afterward, when the Second World War broke out, I was called up for service as a medic. This led to a completely new situation for me and for my future as a moral theologian. I was about to go through some years of a hard education.

CHAPTER 3

TRIAL BY FIRE

Shortly after World War II broke out, I was called up into the army, one of the first priests to be drafted. In keeping with the Concordat, we priests could not be assigned to any fighting units, only to work as medical orderlies. I received my basic training in an army company in Munich that was composed almost exclusively of priests and medical students. Practically every day I celebrated Mass outside the barracks, but to do that I had to disobey orders and take a certain amount of risk. Around the end of November, I went to a newly set up company in Ebingen, not far from Böttingen, my birthplace. In my company there were half a dozen priests. This time we had regular permission to meet every day in the morning in a church for Mass before going on duty.

MY FIRST TEACHING ASSIGNMENT

I was no less surprised when very shortly afterward I was released from service. This release was Father Zettl's doing. He was on friendly terms with the general in charge of the medics, who could properly exempt me in order to work as an academic instructor. Upon my arrival in the seminary, the ailing Father Schmid handed me his textbook and showed me where I could pick up the thread of his lectures. I had the incredible nerve to sketch out immediately my own plan for a whole course in moral theology. I later used this plan as the beginning basis of my work *The Law of Christ*.

At the time Professor Theodore Steinbüchel, who later directed my doctoral thesis, was in hiding in our monastery. He already knew that I had been earmarked as his future doctoral candidate. As far back as those days in 1939, he gave me the topic for my dissertation: "The Holy and the Good: The Reciprocal Relationship Between Religion and Morality." As he explained to me then, "This topic is the subject for Catholic moral theology in the twentieth century. Your work will give you a clear blueprint for your task."

In my lectures I tried to accomplish the impossible: combining my own ideas and viewpoints with the main ideas as they was covered in the Aertnys-Damen textbook. At carnival time, which was often the occasion for practical jokes, my students pulled my leg and claimed that I had invited them to bring the "two ladies" to every class, even though I obviously did not know what to do with them. This joke was based on the fact that the word *"Damen"* in German means "ladies."

The course that I had to give was extremely intensive. I was supposed to prepare the ordination class, which had more than ten men in it, so that they could receive Holy Orders before the summer. Nevertheless, the resulting collaboration was ideal. The seriousness of the situation forced everyone to concentrate on the essentials.

BACK TO SCHOOL AGAIN

Since practically all the students in the summer course of 1940 were called up for military service, my superiors had me matriculate at the University of Tübingen. My first visit there, which I spent listening to Karl Adam, the renowned dogmatic theologian, as well as the moral theologian Otto Schilling, was warmly satisfying. But scarcely had the lectures begun than I received my orders to report to the army again.

I was called up to the school for orderlies in Augsburg. The course was very intensive and oriented to practicality. I threw myself into my medical learning heart and soul, because I realized that the lives of many people might depend upon my competence and skill.

ASSIGNMENT: FRANCE

In 1941, after my medic training, I was sent with a medical company to France, near Bayeux, in Normandy. I was lucky. The chaplain in charge, although it was against regulations, assigned me to military pastoral care. I immediately started saying Mass every Sunday for my medical company and also in the cathedral of Bayeux. In both places the services were jammed.

The second time I rode my bicycle to the cathedral, I happened to run into a colonel, the commandant of the city. He motioned for me to stop. Well, I'm finished, I thought; but it turned out otherwise. The commandant amiably introduced himself (he had already been informed about me by the division chaplain). He asked me whether I had any objections to his delegating the regimental band to accompany the services. In addition, he said he would get someone in my company to bring me by car to say Mass. Anyone who knows the history of Nazism and its antireligious decrees may well be stunned by this blatant act of disobedience— and that nothing happened to us as a result. I believe that this experience sheds some light on attitudes inside the

Wehrmacht. Brave men acted as if they knew nothing about certain decrees of the Hitler regime. And occasionally this "ignorance" went on for a long time.

Every Sunday, the cathedral of Bayeux was filled with soldiers and civilians, mostly French, some of whom were more than a little amazed that anything like this was possible under Hitler. After all, we mere priest/medics had been explicitly instructed about the legal situation. We had been informed precisely how many years in prison were awaiting us should we dare to work as pastors, in any way at all, within the Wehrmacht.

However, as far as I could discover, during the war and afterward, such cases of systematic transgression of the law were relatively rare. A whole series of factors had to coincide. Apart from courage on the part of the priest/medic, it took cooperation from the divisional or army chaplain and the commandant in charge. In my case, during the war years this kind of cooperation took place almost routinely. But in each situation I had to take the initiative myself. Even if some officers were not exactly happy about the turn of events, they knew that their men prized my services and they would make themselves highly unpopular if they tried to stop them.

In the Bayeux region, I came into frequent contact with the civilian population not just through my regular liturgies in the cathedral but also through my work as an interpreter for my unit. This interaction led to the growth of true friendships, both with French priests and with laypeople of the region.

ON THE FRONT IN POLAND

At the beginning of May 1941, our division was shifted to the eastern front, near Sokol and Zamosc in Poland—to a place south of Lublin and not far from the Ukrainian border. As soon as we arrived, my soldier friends built an altar in a large empty barn, where on Sunday I celebrated Mass for my company and all nearby units. Since there was no church there, many Poles also came to Mass, which was still said in Latin. I also accepted invitations from the Poles to celebrate Mass for them.

A certain captain, a devout Nazi, reported me to the regimental commander, not on account of the services for the soldiers, but because of my fraternizing with Polish civilians. There was a formal hearing, where the colonel in charge asked me whether it was true that I had once celebrated Mass together with Poles. I replied, "That is not quite accurate. This happened not once, but many times." Whereupon the colonel asked me, in a measured tone, whether I had anything to say in my defense, suggesting that perhaps that I hadn't known about the regulations in question. My answer was brief. "Might I be allowed to handle my case along with that of the captain who reported me?" The captain happened to be standing nearby. I pointed out that the captain had been getting together with Polish women to drink schnapps, which is, after all, a more serious matter than praying together. The colonel gave the captain an angry look. "Sergeant Häring," he said sternly, "you can go." Then, as I later learned, the colonel seriously chewed out my accuser, who now had become the accused. Word of this got around, and people said, "Don't mess with Häring."

On the eve of the Russian campaign, we were stationed in a sprawling forested area. With the permission of the head of my company and the nearest regimental commander, I celebrated a Mass at dawn with general absolution. Practically everyone attended, both Protestants and Catholics: at a moment like that it would have been absurd to exclude our

Protestant comrades from absolution and communion. Everyone knew how serious our situation was.

HARSH DEMANDS OF BATTLE

Almost immediately afterward the artillery began to blast away on both sides. A grenade landed close by me, directly hitting my nearest neighbor, a Jesuit named Fichter, splitting his steel helmet and tearing his brain to pieces. Just before then, I had been letting my thoughts wander and had said, "Might it not be for the best, if we were to quickly lose this senseless, hopeless war and put an end to our misery?" My friend answered, "I wouldn't want to shed a drop of blood in this criminal war. We will have a large job ahead of us afterward." I gave the dying Jesuit extreme unction. But I soon heard shouts from all sides, "Orderly! Orderly!" I had to clench my teeth to get up the strength to help others. If I had not learned to control my pain, how could I have survived and kept my sanity?

When the war broke out in Russia, I was still in the medical company. Since three more priests had joined us, I volunteered for the medical service in an infantry battalion, where my help was probably most needed. I was immediately transferred as requested, because they were already short on men.

The harsh demands made on an army medic who was at the same time a pastor can be illustrated by the events of a single day. It was in October 1941 in the hard-fought battle that preceded the taking of Kharkov. Early in the morning we attacked superior Russian forces and suffered bloody losses. Among the men who died in my arms was a lad named Bursteiner, who had returned just the day before from the town of Gars on the River Inn. We were in the process of digging in as the Russians launched a massive tank-supported counterattack. Without waiting for orders, our men left the trenches—and so did I, one of the last to go. A Russian tank came plowing right up behind me. The only way I could save myself was to stay so close to it that it could not shoot me but far away enough so that it didn't run over me. Fortunately for us, as we fled, we ran into marshy terrain. We ended up full of mud, but the tanks, which came right after us, ended up sinking into the swamp.

In the next village, we built new lines of defense. I still had not gotten over the panic and fatigue, when wounded soldiers from a neighboring unit came shouting for help. When I tore open the clothes of the first one, his entrails dropped out. I covered them up carefully, and hurriedly expressed my deep regret that I could not help him since he was near death. However, I did ask him if he would let me, as a Catholic priest, say a consoling word or two. The mortally wounded man answered, "I am a Protestant, but if you can say a word of faith for me, I would be grateful." Other soldiers were already screaming for help, so I simply said to him, "God is calling you; he is calling you to himself as a Father. Say yes!" I will never forget his answer, spoken with his last burst of energy, "When God calls, we are always ready." Then I went to attend to four more wounded, and this time I had to say the last good-bye to yet another severely wounded man.

In the afternoon of the same day, we got reinforcements and counterattacked at once. Under fire from Russian tanks and infantry, we had a large number of men killed or badly wounded. In the meantime my four assistants, who were acting as stretcher-bearers, had paid for their helpfulness with their lives. I had to run from one end of the unit to the other. And all this was taking place in open terrain, where we were easy marks for the Russian sharpshooters. Finally, I managed to dig myself a rough-and-ready foxhole, and crawled in, dead tired. But then desperate cries of "Medic! Medic!" rang out from a nearby battalion. I could have given the excuse that this was outside my service area, but I heard the agony in the cries. So I decided to run across the open field to the place where the cries were coming from.

There I found a South Tyroler, horribly wounded in the gut but still conscious. I attended to him as best I could; then I introduced myself as a priest. When he heard that I could give him Communion, his eyes filled with tears and he said in amazement, "How good God is to a poor sinner like me." I was still with him when he drew his last breath. As always in such cases, I copied from his ID card the address of his relatives to send them the dead man's last greeting.

Years later, when I was lecturing in the Tyrol, I met a priest who was a nephew of the fallen soldier. I learned from him that the man had left the Church because of a vehement quarrel with his pastor. His mother had cried her eyes out in deep sorrow, but the young man had not found the inner strength to return to the Church. Still, during this time, he had demonstrated his good will by his continuous generosity to the poor—perhaps earning the grace for a deathbed confession.

BEHIND THE RUSSIAN LINES

Hardly had we marched into Kharkov than I was assigned to go along with seven men on a scouting party almost ten miles behind enemy lines. I was chosen because I spoke Russian, but I called the commander's attention to the fact that I was only a medic. He promptly replied, "Perhaps the seven men on this assignment will need a medic more than an interpreter." To this day, I can still recall every detail of this strange mission. Russian civilians kept warning us when we were getting too close to their own soldiers. How often I experienced something like that in those four terrible years. Many simple people did not think in terms of friend or foe, but just in terms of humanity and compassion.

On this scouting mission, most of the time I rode on my bicycle ahead of the seven others. I did this because I had to ask people for directions. As I was peddling up a steep path, I suddenly found myself facing fifty Russian soldiers, who were marching toward me in strict formation, every one armed with a rifle. What should I do? To my complete surprise I heard myself ordering them, "*Rucki wierch,*" or "Hands up!" in the booming voice I had back then. It worked, and the men all threw their guns away. They must have thought, mistakenly, that this detachment was merely our advance guard. I approached them amiably, and encouraged them to return to their wives and mothers. To do that successfully, I told them to get rid of their uniforms and find some civilian clothes.

I already had some experience with the treatment of Russian soldiers by the German army. Once I had nursed a group of Russian soldiers back to health. According to orders, they were supposed to be led back behind our lines, but an SS officer shot them to death. Afterward I discussed the matter with our divisional commander. The commander had no objections when I told him that, in view of this scandalous crime against international law and humanity, from now on I would advise wounded Russians to find some civilian clothes and head back home.

In the years to come, I would learn from time to time that word had gotten around about my concern for healing Russian prisoners and the civilian population. I once met a

Russian mayor, at whose house I wanted to quarter German and Russian wounded, who told me, "If the Germans would look after Russian prisoners and sick Russian soldiers the way the doctor in Mal Psinka did, you Germans would win the war." Not until a few days later did he learn that I was the "doctor" from Mal Psinka. Though I was only a sergeant in the medical corps, everywhere people called me doctor.

THE HIDDEN WAR AGAINST THE JEWS

In Kharkov, my comrades turned the large movie house on Sumskaya Street into a church. Over a properly constructed altar table hung a beautiful picture of Saint George. Every Sunday the former movie house was filled with soldiers who attended and prized the services. This attendance at Mass made a big impression on the Russian population.

But in Kharkov I also made an altogether horrible discovery. One Sunday I had called together all the priests and religious whom I had gradually gotten to know in Kharkov. We discussed our limited opportunities for active pastoral care. Scarcely anyone had as much freedom as I did. When we parted from one another on the street, I saw a sign in Russian. It ordered all Jews to assemble at a certain place the next morning, with all their luggage, for the purpose of re-settlement. I immediately asked my comrades to return to the house with me. I had already heard credible rumors that Hitler had had tens of thousands of Jews murdered in Kiev. We agreed that before nightfall, we would warn all the Jewish families we knew not to obey this order. We all endeavored to save as many lives as possible by passing along information, though we realized if that word of this action got out, it could endanger our own lives.

Late in the evening on the following day, a soldier from our unit came to me in total confusion. It took a long time before I could get him to talk. He was one of the men who had been detailed to a *Sonderkommando* (special commando) detail. Then suddenly he and his fellows found themselves faced with the criminal task of shooting Jews so that they fell down into the graves they had already dug. The men had been forced to swear beforehand not to say anything about it; they would risk their lives if they did. A few days later yet another soldier spoke with me about this depraved and savage situation. Still, I felt bound by confidentiality not to endanger the two men. The reader can imagine what anger was building up inside of me.

SAVING LIVES

In the spring of 1945, I came very close once again to this inhumanity, the greatest mass crime of our century, the murder of the Jews. One evening I was coming back late to our unit, alone with our battalion doctor, because we had had to take care of the wounded.

Suddenly, we stumbled onto a path and, alongside it, the corpses of women, all shot in the back of the neck. We could still hear the death rattle in some of their throats. No sooner had we rejoined our troops, who were stationed in Großschlewitz, than my comrades came to me. They had watched as hundreds of Hungarian Jewish women were being herded along. Anyone who wouldn't or couldn't keep up with the pace of the forced march was shot, always in the nape of the neck. My friends saw this barbarism and tried to save as many of the women as possible. When the marchers went around a curve, and the guards were out of sight, they took these dead-tired women aside. By the time we arrived, they had already lodged them with Polish families. My friends expected me to look after the women. I visited and cared for them as best I could; but since some of them were very sick, I asked the battalion doctor to visit them. His face turned anxious, and he answered, "My dear friend, you don't have a wife and children. You are only risking your own life. I will gladly stand by and advise you. Unfortunately, I can't do anything more than that."

I was more than a little surprised by the cooperation between German soldiers and Polish families in the attempt to save these Jewish women. Later, I found out that these women had been evacuated from the Stutthoff concentration camp in East Prussia in the face of the approaching Russian army. For an entire week, we were on tenterhooks, as men from the *Sicherheitsdienst* (the security service, or SD) came looking for the hidden Jews.

One morning, the Polish parish priest invited me to breakfast. He himself feared for his life. He had already been in a concentration camp, where he came close to being shot. At that time his life had been saved by a German officer. While we were still sitting over breakfast, an officer from the *Sicherheitsdienst* came in. He demanded that the pastor come with him, claiming that he had to bring him to a safe place, since the Russian army was fast advancing. I immediately saw what that meant. With all my medals on my chest, I jumped into the game, "Give me your name instantly," I roared. "You are a defeatist. Don't you know that our Führer has issued a solemn declaration that the army must not retreat an inch. And now you dare tell this Pole that you have to bring him to where he will be safe from the Russians!" The man was taken aback by my thundering voice and angry face. The pastor was rescued. Shortly afterward, another officer tried to bring the unit chaplain "to a safe place"; so I played the comedy all over again, with the same success.

That very same day the German army retreated, and the Russians occupied the village. Our Hungarian protegees were saved—at least in part by the courageous disobedience of some soldiers of the German Wehrmacht. It is proof of how many men, despite everything, showed conscience and reverence for human life.

In May 1996, I received an interesting visit from an old man. He had read one of my books in which I describe how, in the middle of a harsh winter, my battalion and I were surrounded by the Russian army. There were no transport vehicles left. I absolutely had to get a dozen seriously wounded soldiers to the nearest field hospital—but how could I do this? Since I had also taken a lot of trouble with the sick among the civilian population, the farmers offered to lend me the horses and sleighs that they had kept hidden. It was a bold adventure between the two front lines. Thanks to our Russian guides, we found the place where the field hospital was located. I dropped off the sick and wounded, and was lucky enough to make my way back safely. My visitor explained to me, "Don't you recognize me? I was there. You saved my life back then." Of course, it wasn't me who worked this miracle, but God's providence, along with the help of Russian peasants.

PRIEST TO THE RUSSIAN ORTHODOX

In Russia, I unexpectedly and without any planning became a baptizer. Shortly after the beginning of the war in Russia, I found myself stationed at a house in which three little children lived. When the village came under heavy artillery fire, the mother complained to me that her two smallest children were still unbaptized. She told me how she had taken the oldest boy all the way to Dnepropetrovsk, a city about 180 miles away, to have him baptized. Far and wide there were no priests to be had. So I decided to baptize the two smaller children as solemnly as possible under the circumstances. The villagers did not know that, when necessary, laypeople too can baptize. Needless to say, I baptized these children as Orthodox Christians, for this was the only Church that was their spiritual home. I made the sign of the cross in the manner of the Eastern Orthodox (from right to left instead of from left to right). As a result of these experiences, my way of thinking became far more ecumenical.

As long ago as my time in France, I had regularly held Bible classes for Protestant soldiers. Now the Orthodox Christian world came to the center of my attention. Willy-nilly, the baptizing of Orthodox children in the Ukraine and Russia suddenly became part of my life as a priest. Evidently the word spread all over that I baptized children. In the region of Gomel, the inhabitants of a small town of some ten thousand inhabitants asked me to hold a baptismal ceremony. Since I was staying there for several weeks, I was able to solemnly baptize practically all the children and adolescents up to the age of eighteen—because that was how long these people had gone without a priest. I did everything in Russian, though I had no book to go by. The people were so moved, they wept. I myself got so excited by this great event that I kept having to stop and catch my breath in order not to be overcome by sheer amazement.

In some places, as soon as mothers learned that we were getting ready to move out, they came running to me with their children and begged me to baptize them. Other mothers often cried and complained that they had missed their chance. Perhaps this experience I had of baptism, which I often found so moving, contributed to the fact that in my spirituality and theology, Jesus' baptism in the Jordan—with a view to his baptism in his own blood and to our baptism—occupies such a key position. His baptism is Jesus' self-dedication and his Father's dedication of him in the Holy Spirit to his exalted calling as the nonviolent suffering Servant of God, who subordinates himself to all-embracing peace and reconciliation. As baptized men and women, we take part in that calling.

HEALER TO ALL

In a region where my reputation as a healer had already gotten around, one day I was taken to a woman giving birth. Those seeking my help had told me she was "a sick person." When I saw that she was in labor, I apologized. I said I knew nothing about this sort of thing and told them to fetch the midwife. But the only midwives they had were the grandmothers, and they had already given up on the woman.

The people keep begging me more and more urgently, so I gave the woman an injection, in hopes of restoring her energy. Then I left the room, dripping with sweat. The grandmother followed after me, asking, "Well, *now* will it work?" Suddenly cries of joy came ringing out from the house. A few days later, these good people came to take me on the long trip to the baptismal celebration of little Pyotr. If he is still alive, he would now be fifty-three. How often he must have heard the story of his birth and baptism. The fact that I baptized so many Russian children gives me a very special bond with this nation. I often recall the overflowing love that so often poured forth from them to me.

There were different grounds and backgrounds for my grossly exaggerated fame as a healer, a reputation that preceded me almost everywhere and that my comrades ratcheted to even a higher level. For one thing, there was the connection, so important for Russian believers, between the healer and the man of God, or priest. Trust in the healer is a factor in healing whose importance can scarcely be exaggerated. And then, above all, there was the availability of the first generation of antibiotics, the sulfa drugs. Fortunately, I was always able to get a good supply of these drugs. If I gave a sufficient dose to a Russian who was mortally ill with acute pneumonia, within two days he wasn't just free of fever but in good health. Word of *that* quickly made the rounds, so that I was simply (and wrongly) considered a miracle-working doctor, which in turn had an enormous psychological effect on the people I treated.

Naturally, the fact that I was besieged by Russian patients—though I never neglected my comrades—couldn't escape the notice of the officers. And so it happened that I was formally accused before the divisional commander of wasting valuable German supplies. I knew that this commander had previously served in the SS and had been promoted there. Luckily, I could give a good answer, "First of all, my work makes for good relations with the civilian population. Second, I can prove that I mostly use supplies captured from the Russian army." An inspection showed quite clearly that practically everything I had bore inscriptions in Russian. The commander not only acquitted me but publicly praised the work that I was doing. From that point on, he proved himself in many ways to be my supporter.

In the late fall, when things on the front were quiet, he wanted to send me to an officers' school in order that I might qualify for a promotion. But he accepted my excuse that as a priest I was to be employed only in the medical service.

Meanwhile, my comrades kept getting shot, falling left

and right by my side. Rescuing the badly wounded from the battle lines, which I was duty-bound to do, involved no small risk. Thus I gradually began to feel amazement that, time and time again, I got away with mere scratches.

WOUNDED IN THE RUSSIAN OFFENSIVE

In the beginning of May 1942, there was a great offensive between Kursk and Kharkov. The Russians were now much better prepared than the year before. Our infantry regiment, the well-known List Regiment, got its head bloodied. Within a few hours, I had lost my four stretcher-bearers. Once again, a badly wounded man cried out for a medic. While I was attending to him, I was hit by several fragments of a hand grenade. Since the fighting was at close quarters and we were being carefully observed, no one could come to my aid. After a few minutes, my whole uniform was drenched in blood. I was convinced that my last hour had come, and I resigned myself to the will of God. I tore open my container of material for dressing wounds and tried to apply a bandage around my entire head to stop the bleeding. Fortunately, my comrades carried me back behind the lines.

At the bandaging station, my completely blood-soaked uniform had to be cut open. The Russian woman working at the station broke out into tears. But I got very competent treatment and was taken immediately to a transport of wounded men headed back to Germany. One painful complication of my wound was the total rigidity of my mouth, so that I could neither eat nor drink. But by the time I arrived in the hospital in Dillingen, I could do both.

In the large hospital hall, equipped with many beds, there were more than a few SS soldiers. At first they were obviously disappointed that we men were cared for not by pretty girls but by serious-looking nuns. Still, it was refreshing to see how quickly the head sister won their grateful trust. If somebody let out a curse, you could see his obvious concern, "I hope sister didn't hear that."

After barely a month, I was released on a three-week furlough. Then the first doctor to examine me put me down as ready to return to the front. But the physician of the new unit in Munich was angry about that and got me an extra week of furlough.

After this furlough, I was sent back to Russia to the B 49 (*Beobachtungsabteilung,* or observation department) as a battalion medic. The commander, Colonel Vetter, gave me a welcoming reception and approval for my unauthorized pastoral activity. He himself came to Mass, and his adjutant served as the "altar assistant."

RETREAT FROM STALINGRAD

In the winter, the B 49 was stationed in Voronezh, north of Stalingrad. We belonged to the army of General Friedrich von Paulus, whose forces took Stalingrad and defended it for a long time. It is well known that at a certain point, Paulus came to the realization that Stalingrad could neither be occupied nor permanently defended, and so he was thinking of an orderly retreat. But Hitler determined that under no circumstances would he permit a retreat.

As the encirclement by the Russians grew tighter, and Voronezh, too, was already almost completely surrounded, our commandant Colonel Vetter decided to save the unit by retreating—partly because of all its valuable material, which might prove very useful to the enemy if it fell into its hands. But we quickly came under fire and had to abandon all the equipment anyway. In the end we had no officers with us, just some staff sergeants. But everyone turned to me and asked me to take command, if only because I spoke Russian.

Given the fact that we were only lightly armed and extremely fatigued, the idea of fighting our way back was unthinkable. The alternative that I proposed was to throw away our weapons and appeal to the kindness of the civilian population. The supreme rule was this: no killing and no looting.

SAVED BY THE ENEMY

At the first village where we came to that night and begged our way in, people led me to a wounded German soldier who was being cared for in a makeshift fashion by a peasant family. Several Germans had fallen in or around the village. The good people entreated me to take the wounded man with me. And when they saw that we had already dragged quite a number of wounded men with us, they spontaneously offered to provide them with sleighs and horses. What an incredible testimony to their humanity. I think it was clear proof of the faith of these pious farmers. Their attitude was plain to see, especially when one of our men told them I was a priest. They let me know what path to take through the gorges and ravines so that we could save ourselves, because the region was already under the control of the Soviet army.

We never marched down the roads, but through the woods and the snow-covered fields. Where the snow was deep, we all went in single file. The youngest and strongest took turns stamping down the snow. Most nights we camped in barns. I managed to bring up the rear with sleighs carrying about eighteen wounded men, who were unable to walk. And every night I found a warm room for them in the houses of pious farmers. The cold was often fierce. On the sixth day, we heard cannon fire far off in the west, so we knew we had to be close to the front. The last overnight stay of my wounded men was a moving experience. They were bedded down close to one another on hay and straw and covered with blankets. The people gave us, that is, first of all to the wounded, all the bread and milk they had. Then they ran over to their neighbors and begged more milk for our wounded men.

We said heartfelt good-byes. I had always made it my principle not to introduce myself as a priest, *svyaschenik,* until—if at all—departure time, so as not to try to profit from religion. As we said farewell to this wonderfully kind family, I first asked them, "Just tell us, how did you manage to show so much love to us Germans after all the wrong the Germans have done to you?" The mother of the house answered me with marvelous simplicity, "We pray every day that God will send us our five sons back home safe and sound. They are all serving in the army. But how could we have dared to say this prayer today, if we hadn't thought that your mothers and your wives are praying to the same heavenly Father for exactly the same thing that we are praying for?" That is true faith.

On the following night, we slipped through the front lines and arrived in Kursk. We had no idea, of course, where our officers could be. I absolutely had to report our return to some military authority. Then we had to find a place to put up the men. I was arrested and, after a brief proceeding, condemned to work as a medic in a penal company. That amounted to a death sentence, since penal battalions were thrown wherever the action was hottest, and so purely and simply sacrificed. I was put into solitary confinement in a large building, one that also lodged the command staff. One morning I awoke to find the whole house silent. I managed to get out of my room and found the same silence far and wide. It was clear that the German army had charged headlong out of Kursk. I could see that fact just from the chaos in which I found everything. At dusk, I crept out on the way to the west along narrow streets and quiet roads, always following the stars. The next morning, I ran into German units that were digging into new positions. Before nightfall, I found my old unit and was welcomed with jubilation.

FALSE JUDGMENT

For a long time, the B 49 was stationed near Orel. In short order, I had once again become a much-sought-after healer and baptizer for the civilian population. At this point, I only want to tell one story—a story that covered me with shame. I was billeted in a spacious house that belonged to a fine family. They had also offered shelter in a storeroom or anteroom to a woman named Natasha and her four children. Before long, I couldn't help noticing that in order to prevent her children from starving she was working as a prostitute for German soldiers.

I spoke kindly to her and promised her that I would see to it that her children did not go hungry. I could do that since my Russian patients were forever offering me every conceivable kind of food. My assistant chased off all the soldiers who wanted to go on exploiting Natasha. She showed her gratitude for this, for example, by cleaning up all the dirt in the house. Three days before Easter, Natasha explained to me that now she had to concentrate entirely on patching the clothes for herself and her children to wear to church on Easter. Then the nasty words escaped my lips, "What, you go to *church*?" Natasha got the point and broke down crying. I made a full apology.

For Easter she received eggs for herself and the children to have them blessed in church according to the custom. Then she gave one to me with her heartfelt Easter greeting. To this day, I feel so sorry that for a moment when I played the Pharisee with Natasha. How hard it is to drive that spirit out of us!

CHAPTER 4

EXPERIENCING DIVINE PROVIDENCE

I think that for all eternity, I will never get over my wonderment of the mystery of God's loving providence and how it sets us on the path to freedom. God's providence gives us the most fruitful thoughts and, perhaps, at crucial junctions, seems to toss out our plans precisely when and where the meaning, direction, and peculiar quality of our calling is at stake. When I think of all the dangers I faced in the Second World War, I am not just surprised at my own survival, I am astounded. I also wonder at how every event and every person taught me a lesson, so that I could passionately commit my life to the service of healing, liberating nonviolence, to the constructive struggle against war and for the causes of peace, reconciliation, and understanding among nations.

GOD'S BLESSINGS AT WORK

Accidents are so-called, only because we do not give credit to Divine Providence. In my life, and merely to enable me to survive in one piece, so many things had to came together that I have to think the all-wise Master Architect must have been behind it all. God does not keep us in training wheels forever.

His providence does not tie us down in passive helplessness, but gives us abundance and creativity. Just how God's providence, human freedom, and meaningful planning work together is part of the realm of unfathomable mysteries. But we cannot fail to see and hear the workings of providence in our life.

As I see it, the senseless war, which was instigated by Hitler and made possible to begin with by various forms of collective and personal egoism, means that I have to cry out unceasingly with everything that I am and know, "No more wars, ever! Be creative in the struggle against the insane forces of the lust for power and domination! Fight with all your experience and wisdom against the madness of violence and deceit."

How many things, events, and decisions combined together so that I could emerge from the chaos of the war safe and sound and with a clear mission? In praise of Divine Providence, I will recount what happened to me around the end of the war and immediately afterward.

Where did I get the strength to march an average of twenty-five miles a day in a retreat that lasted for weeks and, at the same time, work intensively for the health and life of many other people? What was the source of the inner energies that came pouring into me, so that amid all this I did not lose faith in life or even in the God of love? One great help here was the rich experience of love, friendship, and shared responsibility on the part of men and women tested by pain. In my deepest distress, the trusting prayer of surrender to God's saving plan was an anchor for me.

FLEEING TO DANZIG

Now a brief history of the last weeks before the end of the war: We had gotten to Danzig, with no prospects of continuing our march to the west. Some units were scattered during our hasty flight, because the retreat was now just a desperate, helter-skelter race. The higher command reacted to this senselessly and heartlessly. Anyone who was tracked down and caught separated from his unit could expect to be hanged on the spot without a trial. On the Danzig-Zoppot-Oliva Avenue, on almost every large tree, I saw German soldiers hanged, each bearing a sign around his neck: "I refused to fight." Around that time, I happened to run into Alfons Flad, a nephew of Johannes Flad, whom I have already mentioned and with whom I grew up. Alfons asked me, "Can you try to get me into your unit? It wasn't my fault, but I have lost my unit." I had a better idea. I knew that in a few hours the last hospital ship would be sailing out of the harbor to the west. I put a thick bandage around a slight wound he had and got him taken aboard ship with other sick and wounded soldiers. It worked. In the west he was imprisoned by the English, but very shortly afterward released and sent home.

Our B 49 unit headed out of Danzig for the mouth of the Weichsel River. There we got on a ferry, which normally served to cross the river. Many of us had only a narrow spot on deck on which to stand. We sailed toward the harbor of Hel on Patucka Bay, about twenty-five miles away. Russian planes were flying overhead. But because of a violent storm and the resulting bad visibility, the Russian planes could not sink us. Whenever a powerful wave rolled over the ferry, you could hear screams. A few men were swept overboard and sank into the sea.

MASQUERADING AS A POLISH PASTOR

On the long but narrow Hel Peninsula, German soldiers by the tens of thousands were crammed together, with nothing to look forward to except to end up being captured. We were camping out in a huge stretch of wooded country. By contrast, my section physician, Dr. Wegemann, was quartered in the little town of Heisternest, called Jastarnia in Polish. Armed with a special ID card issued by him, I could move back and forth between the forest camp and Jastarnia, in continual collaboration with my section physician. Dr. Wegemann also agreed to allow me to use my ID to make contact with the parish in Jastarnia.

Since the priest there had been abducted, the sacristan, Alfons Konke, was the representative with whom I dealt. His father was the former mayor. I said Mass for the Polish-Kashubian population at their request. Along with their Kashubian dialect, almost all of the members of the parish in Jastarnia spoke both Polish and German. They also asked me to visit their sick, since they had no doctor. As well, I baptized the children of the parish, including a few illegitimate ones. Thus in the few weeks before the final surrender and capture of the German troops, I developed a cordial friendship with the core of the parish of Jastarnia.

Soon after the German surrender, which turned the Hel Peninsula into a giant POW camp, Alfons Konke and two other men from the parish council showed up to visit me in the bunker. They took me aside and informed me that the parish had decided to keep me on as their pastor. They had even brought along a proper cassock. But they agreed with my request that I first discuss the matter with my best friends from the B 49 unit. And *they* unanimously agreed that I should accept the offer. After all, they pointed out, it wasn't very likely that we would be staying together in captivity. So I changed my clothes and, dressed like a priest and with a Polish ID card, I marched past the camp sentry to Jastarnia, where I moved in with the Konke family.

I immediately took up my priestly duties. On Sundays the large church was full to bursting. After the end of services, Mr. Konke said, "Today everyone in church was nervous—except you." I had memorized some words of greeting in Polish and had evidently carried off my little speech well. Soon I also took up the work of pastoral care in Kusniza (Kußfeld). Every two weeks, I said an additional Sunday Mass there. The local commandant, a devout Orthodox Christian, got in touch with me and gave his men time off on Sunday so that they also could go to Mass. They came in goodly numbers and their behavior was exemplary.

My biggest surprise came when the Russian commandant of Jastarnia decided to set up his headquarters in, of all places, Alfons Konke's house. Mr. Konke observed laconically, "You are safest in the lion's den"—and so I was. During the whole time up to the day of my departure in the autumn of 1945, I never had any serious troubles with the Russians.

HEADING HOME TO BÖTTINGEN

At the time, there was still no mail service to West Germany. So I had no way to write to my parents that I was still alive. My parents' golden wedding anniversary was coming up in October. The thought that when they celebrated this wonderful event they wouldn't even know that I was alive visibly preoccupied me. In the meantime, the real pastor of Jastarnia, though a very sick man, had returned, and, fatherly friend that he was, I first disclosed to him my intention of returning home. He and everyone else was stunned, and they begged me to stay. On the other hand they could readily understand my reasons for wanting to go. In the end, Alfons Konke and his father saw to it that I got traveling papers and recommendations. The whole parish council accompanied me as far as Gdynia and would not leave until I was seated in the train to Stettin. There were many tears all around.

True, I, like the other passengers in the Stettin train, was robbed by a bunch of Russian soldiers; but even after all sorts of other perils I arrived safely in Berlin, where I found a Redemptorist monastery. My fellow religious provided me with official permission from the authorities for a trip to Heiligenstadt im Eichsfeld. There, too, I was given the heartiest sort of reception. My brethren attempted to pull all the wires that they could to find out the place where a German traveler could pass over the demarcation line, without being checked, into the English or the American occupation zone. The results were totally negative. The border was hermetically sealed at every point.

But I knew my arrival would give my parents great joy; and so, although my brethren kept advising me against it, I set off on my journey, wearing a cassock, with no luggage, just a breviary in my hand. In this fashion, I marched past the first Russian border sentry. He obviously took me to be a local priest and let me through without checking my ID. After a while, a farmer amicably invited me to jump up on his hay wagon. I sank into the hay completely out of sight. And so we passed the second border sentry.

But at the third and last checkpoint things were destined to get serious. To my astonishment, one of the two guards was snoring away, sound asleep. I showed the other guard my safe-conduct from Jastarnia, which was written in Russian, in the hope that he would not read it too carefully. But he did, and he politely said to me in Polish, "This won't do. This safe-conduct is valid only for Berlin." But since he spoke Polish, I breathed a sigh of relief and began to converse with him, on and on, until there was nobody else in sight. The amiable fellow had already explained to me in

EXPERIENCING DIVINE PROVIDENCE

some detail that he would be risking a long prison sentence if he were to let me pass with these inadequate papers.

The other guard was still asleep. All at once I thanked the guard in good Polish for letting me cross. I took the risk of walking right through, and he didn't bother to call me back. Once I had reached open country, I sang out loud the hymn, "Great God, we give thee praise."

Then I made my way to the border post of the American zone. There only one soldier was on duty, flirting with an elegant young woman. He was obviously irritated by my showing up. Of course, he could not read my Polish ID nor the Russian safe-conduct pass, but he demanded a German personal ID or a certified permission for crossing the border between the occupation zones. All my urging inspired only the dry response, "Back!" When I didn't budge, he began to fire his rifle over my head. At that point, of course, I disappeared.

Crossing Into the English War Zone

I now found myself in the triangle between the Russian, English, and American zones. So I took the road to the English border post. The guard there was exactly the opposite of the American. He asked me courteously whether I was a Jesuit. I answered in English that I was a Redemptorist, assuming that the word would be absolutely alien to him. "Oh," he replied cheerfully, "the Redemptorists are my best friends." When I arrived at the border point, the two English border guards were engaged in a lively discussion with some women and their children. The women told me that they had bribed the Russian director of the border police with alcohol. He had consented to let them pass out of pity for the children. Then he had seen to it that the dangerous Russian sentry was given a large supply of vodka, with which he drank himself under the table. That solved the puzzle of what they were doing there. I then persuaded the English guard to let the women through (their homes were in the West), even though their papers did not quite add up. And he did, so it was once again time for me to intone "Great God."

After a long walk, I arrived at the Göttingen train station, dead-tired. A man came up to me and cheerfully asked, "You seem to be very tired and hungry, am I right?" I said yes and told him about my trip. He very kindly got me a good meal. Still more, he bought me a ticket to Stuttgart. Overjoyed, I found myself sitting on the right train. But at the zonal border there was once again a painfully exact check of all papers by the Americans. Along with many others, I was taken off the train and directed to a train returning to Göttingen. But then I saw a mother with a small child begging one of he American soldiers to let her travel on. The soldier disappeared; before long his superior officer showed up and put the woman on the right train. So I plucked up my courage and briefly told him my story. And I, too, was allowed to continue my journey into the American zone.

BACK WITH THE REDEMPTORISTS

Late in the evening, the train stopped in Hünefeld, only sixty miles south of Göttingen, and no train was scheduled to leave until the next morning. Introducing myself as a Redemptorist, I asked a passerby the way to the Oblate monastery. A woman on the other side of the street heard me and came rushing up to me, "Do you know that the Redemptorist Father Fries is serving here in the hospital? He'll surely be glad to take you in." And he was. God, how wonderful are your ways.

The next day I was in Stuttgart-Botnang with my brethren, who greeted me with a storm of affection. They immediately helped me to get the necessary papers for the French zone, where my parents lived. While waiting, I visited my sister Hilariona, a Franciscan nun in Göppingen. I had a special reason for getting in touch with her there. On no fewer than three occasions during the four years I was in Russia, my sister and, still more, her superior had sent me the necessary equipment (for example, a chalice) for celebrating the Eucharist after I had lost everything. My sister welcomed me with a cry of joy: "How happy Papa will be," whereupon I knew that my mother was no longer alive.

HOME AT LAST

Within a few days, I had my necessary papers and could set off on the way home. After the long march from the Spaichingen station, I went, first of all, to the cemetery, to visit the grave of my beloved mother. Then I went to surprise my father; his joy and amazement were great. It was a rainy October day with the wind blowing hard; that evening the bells rang out for the rosary. Father quickly got ready to go. When I protested, "Papa, in this weather you just can't go." His answer was firm—and beautiful: "In the beginning of October, I made a resolution to pray the rosary every evening for your return. Now it is time to say thanks." We went together, to thank Providence for being so kind.

But back then *I* wanted to go back to taking providence into my own hands and making my own plans. Just after arriving in Stuttgart, I had written to the provincial, "Thank God, I am alive and in good health. But, please, forget about making me a professor of moral theology. I want to be a missionary. I'm ready right now to preach a mission—that is why I'm waiting in the monastery in Stuttgart for my assignment." The answer came to Böttingen, where I was spending a week. As a matter of fact, I *was* given an assignment to preach a mission in the Stuttgart area. The provincial wrote that he fully understood my request. He did not want to try convincing me to take up my studies again. So I preached a two-week mission, with enthusiasm both on my part and on the part of the parish. Now I felt I was moving full steam ahead on my chosen path.

STUYDING AT TÜBINGEN

But then I received a letter from the rector of the house of studies in Gars, bidding me find a an apartment in Tübingen immediately and to prepare to do my Ph.D. This letter reawakened the old "rascal" in me. I knew that Tübingen was the garrison town for the French occupying forces. Obviously, I would never find a free apartment there. So I presented myself to the parish priest and asked him for a written confirmation that, for the time being, there was no suitable apartment for me in Tübingen. "I can't do that," he told me. "This morning two women, both respected parishioners, came to me and said, 'If any priest who is a student and who needs an apartment arrives, send him to me.' So go first to Mrs. Gebhart. If you don't like the room there, then try Mrs. Schmidt." I saw this as a sign from Divine Providence, and now said yes in my heart to my future calling as a teacher of moral theology.

In the meantime my friend Theodore Steinbüchl had become professor of moral theology in Tübingen. He was very glad when I presented myself, and he immediately recalled the topic he had once had in mind for me, "The Holy and the Good."

I signed up for lectures or seminars with three professors on the Protestant faculty: Adolph Köberle, Heinz Richter, and Helmut Thielicke. For my dissertation on "The Holy and the Good," I thoroughly studied the Catholic thinker Max Scheler, the atheistic disciple of Husserl Nikolai Hartmann, the two classic Protestant thinkers Kant and Theodore Schleiermacher, and a man highly esteemed in those days, Emil Brunner. Steinbüchl was happy to see the ecumenical orientation and breadth of my research. And he was more than a little surprised when, as early as January 1947, I handed him the finished manuscript for its first presentation. He read it and approved it without any reservations. "Of course," he observed, "I noticed that your criticism of those who stress moral perfection has me among its targets. But your critique makes sense."

In June 1947, I took the final oral examination—still quite rigorous back then—in the presence of the entire faculty. On each of the eight main subjects, I was questioned for half an hour by the professor whose field it was: four hours with only a brief recess, as the old Tübingen regulations demanded.

After I had passed the exam and was declared a Doctor of Theology, I invited my thesis advisor, Professor Theodore Steinbüchl, to a lavish lunch at the home of my landlady, Mrs. Gebhart. My father provided all the food. The meal really did the professor good (he had been used to starvation fare in the French occupying zone), while he expressed his amazement that, after going through my ordeal, I could eat with such gusto. My appetite was unimpaired, for it had been a friendly group of examiners. Before the examination, Professor Karl Adam had told his colleagues, "I insist on treating Father Häring not as a student, but as a colleague."

Now I was clearly in the place where Divine Providence had wanted me to be. Theodore Steinbüchl dared to predict that I would surely make an important contribution to the much-needed renewal of Catholic moral theology. I found his confidence in me enormously encouraging.

TEACHING AT GARS AM INN

Immediately after taking my degree, I reassumed my teaching chores at the Redemptorist theological college in Gars am Inn. By 1948, I began to get a clearer view of my future field of concentration. Our superior general Leonardus Buys, a former professor of moral theology himself, called me to Rome for consultation about his great plan. He wanted to create an institute for the training of future moral theologians, first of all for our own congregation, but then for the entire Church. He was very concerned about the fact that many bishops or superiors of religious orders sent their moralists-to-be off to Rome to specialize in canon law and then have them teach moral theology. In this way, Catholic morality was taken over, so to speak, by institutionalized legalism. We agreed that biblical theology and the social sciences had to be an indispensable foundation for a specifically Christian moral teaching. A series of discussions took place. Father Buys invited me to take a look at the theological faculties in Rome to see how morality was taught there.

The most influential and best-known moralist in Rome at that time was undoubtedly Father F. X. Hürth, S.J., who taught at the Gregorian University. So I went there amid a throng of hundreds of students to study at his feet. He was lecturing on an important *casus,* or case: Is a priest allowed to say two Masses on workdays, if otherwise a group of believers would go an entire year without getting the chance to attend Mass?" His solution was straightforward, "At no time and in no place has there been a law requiring attendance at

Mass on weekdays. Hence, there is no reason for saying two Masses on a weekday."

I looked around the lecture hall to see how the students would react. They were all listening in docile silence, so I took my hat and quietly walked out of the hall. That, I thought, must be the limit—to regard the Eucharist purely from the standpoint of a legal requirement. And as if that were not enough, Father Hürth was one of the most prominent advisors of the Holy Office. Did I need any clearer proof of the need for an academy for the thoroughgoing renewal of Catholic moral theology?

Now I saw my calling: to teach moral theology in Rome and to work with others to found the Academia Alfonsiana. Today that school can look back on almost fifty years of history. More than three thousand men and women students from all over the world, including non-Catholics, did graduate work there so as to become specialists in moral theology.

AT WORK IN ROME

To my good fortune, the transition to my teaching activity in Rome took place step by step. From 1950 to 1953, I spent one semester every year in Rome. The rest of the time I taught in Gars on the Inn and worked on my three-volume work of moral theology *The Law of Christ*, whose first edition appeared in Germany in 1954. When Father Buys died in 1953, the new leadership of the order decided to suspend operations in Rome for a few years, so as to put together a competent faculty. That meant I could for the moment remain rooted in Germany. I did specialized work in pragmatically oriented sociology of religion and helped out with a new type of regional mission by doing sociological research and giving many courses.

In addition, I found a fascinating new field of work:

collaboration with the labor unions. Shortly after the publication of *The Law of Christ,* I was invited by the Protestant Academy in Tutzing to be one of the speakers at a conference, at which leading members of both union and management associations met to deal with burning issues of the post-war economy.

I was quite surprised when, after giving my first paper, the main speaker suggested that we switch roles. I would deliver the six basic presentations and he would respond to them, so as to create a basis for fruitful discussions. I had to give in to the pressure, and I tried to do my best. I received no invitations from the management side. But from then on the DGB (*Deutscher-Gewerkschaftbund,* the Alliance of German Unions) regularly invited me to give courses for their top leadership people. I felt very good doing this work, and could never get over the many signs of sympathetic understanding I received from the union leaders.

When the Church made an attempt to create its own Christian labor unions, I came out strongly for a single unified labor organization, so that Christian workers would not remain or become "a little pile of salt next to the soup bowl," but continue as creative collaborators within the union movement as a whole. When I got a permanent call to Rome, it was not easy to give up my work with the union alliance. However, much to my astonishment, I was soon "discovered" in Rome by the Italian union associations and maintained a fruitful interaction with them.

Europe

View of Father Häring's birthplace, Böttingen in the Bavarian Alps

Church in Böttingen where Father Häring was baptized

Parish church at Jastarnia in Poland where Father Häring served as pastor at the end of World War II

Graduation from *Gymnasium* at Günzburg. Father Häring is in
back row, fourth from left

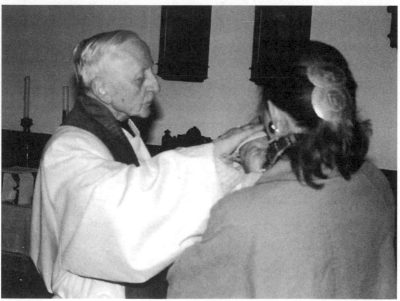

Conferring the sacrament of baptism

Celebrating the Holy Eucharist

Father Häring, seated, first row left, with fellow faculty members at the Academia Alphonsiana, Rome, 1969

Father Häring with two of his brothers and a sister, 1967, from left to right, Martin, Sister Lucidia, Wenzel, and Father Häring

Four of Father Häring's sisters, from left to right, Sister Hilaronia, Sister Rose, Maria Ursula, and Sister Lucidia

Father Häring's cousin (left), Georg Kiesinger, former Chancellor of
West Germany

With a former classmate from 1933

With a new generation

Feeding a furry friend

CHAPTER 5

WORKING TOGETHER TO RENEW MORAL THEOLOGY

A short time ago, I received a visit from three former students of the Academia Alfonsiana, one of whom was an Italian woman theologian. The talk turned to what they considered the specific and identifying features of my moral theology. The Italian theologian gave an extemporaneous summary. She described my moral theology as "thoroughly ecumenical, thoroughly therapeutic, and, above all, focused on the healing power of nonviolence." She also saw it as "marked by the centrality of peace with a view to the nonviolent Servant of God, Jesus; marked by the primacy of joyful faith and the basic decision for God; and marked by the primacy of the 'goal commandments' over the 'limit commandments.'" She hadn't worked this description up beforehand; it came out quite spontaneously. This visit and discussion brought back memories of my early days at the Academia Alfonsiana.

In 1950, when I began to teach at the Academia Alfonsiana, I was already hard at work on the preparation of the manuscript on moral theology that would come to be called in English, *The Law of Christ*. Dialogue with my colleagues, as well as access to the best libraries in Rome, was a great help.

SERVING THE ECUMENICAL IDEAL

In the first year at the Academy, I offered two courses. One course was titled "Repent and Believe in the Gospel," and it treated the topic of fundamental and lasting conversion as a dynamic element of the whole body of Christian morality. This course got an enthusiastic reception from everyone who took it. I taught a second course on the ecumenical orientation of all moral theology, with the title "What Can Catholic Moral Theology Learn From the Orthodox and the Reformation Churches?" This course, too, met with a strong positive response, although it did run into objections.

The abrupt transition from narrow Catholic polemics or apologetics to a readiness to learn from non-Catholics stirred up anxiety in certain people. They simply were not accustomed to speaking of other parts of Christendom except in an apologetic-defensive manner. One of them even asked, "Isn't Father Häring a crypto-Protestant?" I also had suggested to my students that they take Professor Stanislas Lyonnet's courses on biblical ethics at the Biblicum, and those who did found that Lyonnet and I were headed in the same direction along parallel tracks. Still, I decided to drop my ecumenical course on Catholic moral theology for the time being. I decided that my message had to be inserted into the curriculum in a more gentle fashion.

Despite this postponement, my ecumenical theme and focus stayed with me, and, in fact, it became more and more a key structural element in my whole moral theology. My ecumenical stance gradually found a clear echo among others as well. Here is one example. At an ecumenical gathering in the United States, the subject of the ecumenical focus of my moral theology came up. One American theologian said he found it difficult to incorporate my approach into his thinking. A Patriarch of the Eastern Church responded to this statement by saying, "We don't have that sort of difficulty. We look on Father Häring as one of us." That was far too high praise for me; but at the same time, it was also a great incentive.

Early on in my years of teaching and writing, an Anglican bishop had written in the *London Times* that through my contribution to a renewal of moral theology based on the Bible and on salvation history, I had swept away a major obstacle to ecumenism. That outcome, indeed, was what I was concerned about in all my efforts. But whatever serves the ends of ecumenism is, at the same time and above all, a blessing for the catholicity of our Church. A mutual readiness to learn brings mutual enrichment.

LEARNING FROM ALL

Looking back now, I see it as providential that right from the start, in Tübingen, I had continually been concerned with knowing more about the best Protestant theology. My pronounced enthusiasm for Orthodox theology and spirituality is rooted in my pastoral involvement with the Orthodox Christians of Russia during the war. But I have also taken pains to study Orthodox theology and tradition as carefully as possible. As I did, I always had the feeling that this was an inner enrichment of genuine catholicity. In this respect, the Second Vatican Council was a powerful motivating force for me and for many bishops and theologians. I found a refreshing "catholic" quality and ecumenical fervor in particular during my many meetings with the two theologians from Taizé, Brother Robert Schutz and Brother Max Thurian. Pope

John had specifically invited them to the Council, and their spirituality and ecumenical zeal proved to be contagious in the very best sense.

During the Council, Patriarch Maximus Saigh, who remained conscientiously loyal to Orthodox theology and spirituality, chose me as one of his theological advisers. And a spark seemed to shoot from him to me. Again, during the Council, the venerable patriarch Athenagoras of Constantinople kept in touch with me through a journalist who was in Rome for the Council and who served as a kind of postman delivering commentary between Pope Paul VI and his sponsor Athenagoras. I once got a passionate letter from Athenagoras that I was asked to read in the presence of this particular journalist, who could thus vouch to the patriarch for the depth of my commitment. In it, the ardent promoter of the reunion of the Churches urged me to do everything humanly possible to help the Latin Church better understand and appreciate the idea of *oikonomia*, so characteristic of Orthodox spirituality. The idea of *oikonomia* is, applied, above all, to the pastoral care of divorced couples. However necessary the reunion of the Orthodox Churches with Rome might be, the patriarch could not even think of a reunion if Rome brought a harsh, legalistic attitude to bear on the thought and practice of the Orthodox.

I took that very much to heart, and since then I have put a much stronger and more thorough emphasis on the primacy of grace over the law in morality and in pastoral care. To this day, I have had all kinds of problems with Roman Catholic churchmen, who are "Roman" through and through, with no awareness at all of the riches that the Eastern churches in particular possess.

My book *No Way Out? Pastoral Care of the Divorced and Remarried* was a part of my effort to keep the promise I made to the patriarch. Later, Bishops Lehman of Mainz, Saier of Freiburg, and Casper of Rottenburg-Stuttgart dared to take a cautious step toward the spirituality and practice of *oikonomia*—though still entirely within the Catholic Church's tradition of *epikeia*—in their pastoral letter on caring for divorced and remarried Catholics. For their trouble they were dealt a body blow by the Vatican. Did the people in the Vatican realize how deeply these issues affect reunion and reconciliation with the Orthodox?

Here I touch on one of the points with which some Western bishops, theologians, and canonists have an unusually hard time. They do not seem to have any feel for the fact that ecumenical enthusiasm goes hand in hand with a willingness to rethink the position of our own Church.

ECUMENICAL CONTACTS

My contacts with the Reformation Churches, both during and after the Second Vatican Council, were manifold and sustained. In most cases, I did not, at first, take the initiative. These contacts simply came my way, a pure gift. The observers from these Churches, who lived through the Council and even partly helped to shape it, arranged many invitations for me to the United States and to the U.K. I was a visiting professor for a semester at a series of respected Protestant faculties: at Brown University, Yale Divinity School, and Union Theological Seminary in New York. In addition, I gave so many short courses or guest lectures at other Protestant divinity schools that it would be impossible to list them completely. I was also invited to speak by Oxford and other English universities. Everywhere I went I felt the happy wafting of the spirit of friendship, of reciprocal trust, and shared zeal for the testament of Jesus, "That all may be one."

Ecumenical activity on the academic and scholarly level also led to the blossoming of pastoral work. At the three American schools I mentioned previously, ecumenical prayer circles sprang up spontaneously. The initiative generally did not come from me, but from the students or professors. Thanks to Dr. Douglas Steere, the Quaker observer at the Council, the Church of the Savior, which has branches in Baltimore and Washington, D.C., and which was strongly supportive of ecumenism, took notice of me. Until I had my larynx removed, I used to give spiritual exercises every year in their retreat center at Dayspring, where I surely received as much as I was able to transmit to others.

In Dunblane, Scotland, later the scene of a shocking massacre of school children, I was invited by the leadership of the Church of Scotland for two weeks of theological dialogue, which led to deep spiritual reflection and encouragement for all of us.

In 1980, in the Starnberg clinic, when I was allowed to receive visitors after my surgery, the Protestant town pastor was the first to arrive. He brought me a wonderful bouquet from his wife and reminded me of the spiritual exercises that she had made with me years before.

Professor Helmut Thielicke, whose lectures I attended in Tübingen, has repeatedly visited me. After all I have seen, I dare to say that my relationship to the Church is ecumenically Catholic. I can no longer imagine how one could be genuinely Catholic without being marked by Jesus' prayer, "That all may be one." And I am confident that I was allowed to make my small contribution to the fact that the most important sign of the renewal in Catholic moral theology is its dynamic ecumenism.

During my many contacts with believers, and even with bishops, from other Churches, I frequently could not help being amazed at their zeal for the cause of Christian unity. I recall, for example, conversations with Archbishop Michael Ramsey of Canterbury. When he met Pope Paul VI in Rome, the pope had placed the so-called "ring of the fisherman" on his hand. Later he asked me how this gesture should be interpreted. I expressed my conviction that it was a meaningful prophetic gesture, plainly demonstrating that the bishop of Rome truly recognized the bishop of Canterbury as a bishop. In my view it was the strongest sign of hope that the question of the validity of Anglican orders would find a simple solution.

In his book *Moral Theology After the Council: People, Programs, Positions* (Göttingen, 1987), the Protestant theologian Wolfgang Nesthöfel gives an overview of postconciliar Catholic theology in the German-speaking world. Pages 25 to 77 offer an accurate acknowledgment of my own work. Ecumenical interests were never a mere accessory in the development of my moral theology; they were always an essential dimension. For me this is an extra-special motive to thank God for my calling as a moral theologian.

CHRIST AT THE CENTER

Christocentrism is a key concern of all my efforts in reforming moral theology. It finds increasingly clear expression in my two main works, *The Law of Christ* (translated into at least twelve languages) and *Free and Faithful in Christ* (translated into almost as many). The basic question is, In what perspective do I see Jesus of Nazareth? My answer is this: He is for me the Son of man, which means above all that he is "one of us." He is the Son of God, the Father's unsurpassable offering and assent to us. He is the prophet, the nonviolent, but also powerful, unmasker of all false images of God, of every religious falsification, the perfect worshiper in spirit and in truth.

Still another vital perspective for me and my theological efforts is Jesus' baptism in the Jordan. There we see his dedication of himself, solemnly confirmed by his Father, as the absolutely nonviolent Servant of God prophesied by Second Isaiah. He paves the way and shows us the path of peace, the path that leads to baptism in his own blood on the wood of the cross, where in his last "*Abba*-prayer" ("Father, forgive them," Lk 23:34; "Father, into your hands I commend my spirit," Lk 23:46), he clearly reveals his crucial program of peace for his disciples.

HEALING POWER OF NONVIOLENCE

I believe that it is now high time to make every exertion so that all Christians may see their calling as baptized believers in the light of the nonviolent Servant of God. We have to put everything on the line so that they dedicate themselves completely to this peace-program of active, creative nonviolence, so that they study and practice it in all its dimensions. Its modern-day models are, among others, Mahatma Gandhi, Martin Luther King, Jr., and, not least of all, Dietrich Bonhoeffer. When Gandhi died at the hand of a murderer, one Indian Catholic bishop said: "The greatest Christian of our time has died." He had not received the Christian rite of baptism, of course. But his thinking, feeling, and actions were thoroughly immersed in Jesus' baptismal calling and his final "*Abba*" on the cross.

During the Second Vatican Council, as the secretary elected to edit the great document *Gaudium et Spes* (*The Pastoral Constitution on the Church in the Modern World*), I worked tirelessly to include in it a very strong and unequivocal statement on the Christian's calling to peace—meaning nonviolence. I was constantly spurred ahead in this effort by the Quaker Dr. Douglas Steere, by Hildegard and Jean Goss-Meier, and other apostles of peace. It was clear to us that the "signs of the time" with regard to peace and the renunciation of the evil spirit of violence had in fact already become signal fires.

In what was probably the critical study conference in Zurich, convened to plan our work on *Gaudium et Spes,* I emphasized a viewpoint strongly oriented to salvation history, in keeping with the "signs of the time." Despite all the resistance from the static- and scholastic-minded churchmen, this viewpoint prevailed. It finds particularly clear expression in the fifth chapter of *Gaudium et Spes,* "The Fostering of Peace and the Promotion of a Community of Nations" (n. 77–90). The most important text puts it this way: "Animated by the same Spirit, we cannot deny recognition to those who, while guarding their rights, renounce the use of force....Insofar as people are united in love and thus overcome sin, they also overcome violence, until the words of the prophet (Isa 2:4) are fulfilled: 'They shall beat their swords into plowshares, and their spears into pruning hooks; nation shall not lift up sword against nation, neither shall they learn war anymore'" (*Gaudium et Spes,* n. 78).

I have given countless lectures, sermons, and conferences, and written many articles on the healing and liberating power of nonviolence. Perhaps one of my most significant books is published on this topic and is entitled *The Healing Power of Peace and Nonviolence*—a book that has been published in a number of languages.

Over time, it became increasingly clear to me that our struggle for a nonviolent culture of peace presupposes that before all else we must cultivate the attitude of nonviolence in ourselves. We have to forgive others (and ourselves) from

the heart, and ban all loveless thoughts. More than just for-
giving people, we must make them capable, in healing and in
nonviolent love, of becoming friends of ourselves and of others. It gives me great gladness that my efforts on behalf of a
culture of nonviolence were well received by the Catholic
organization *Pax Christi* in Italy, Germany, and France.

Looking back on my life, I think I can see an infinitely
kind Divine Providence at work. It prepared me, above all
through the cruel—and occasionally liberating—experiences
of World War II for my task as a voice calling out for comprehensive nonviolence. If this autobiography were to stimulate
anyone to devote himself or herself to the cause of nonviolence, then it was worth every ounce of my effort.

LEGALISTIC BLOCKS TO FAITH

From my experience as a pastoral caregiver, I became more
and more aware that a moral doctrine totally shaped by law
(or, worse yet, shaped by the kind of law that is forever drawing uncrossable boundaries) does not even serve the law, much
less the joy of the Lord. An often meaningless fixation on
banal legalistic distinctions leads to spiritual poverty, to a
cramped and even sick state of mind. It blocks the joy of
faith, which is after all our true strength.

Here let me point out an especially typical feature of
this mentality. The casuistic manuals of ethics that were still
in vogue when I began to teach moral theology treated, for
example, the topics of the commandments and laws before
mentioning grace and the sacraments. After the long and
detailed presentation of the many laws that were binding
"under mortal sin," the sacraments were introduced in the
following manner: "We need grace so that we can keep all
the commandments and laws."

But this order of presentation was getting everything backward, completely distorting the fundamental truth that we live as Christians in the "law of grace." Our grateful yes to the order of grace, our jubilation over the Good News, is the most precious fountain of youth that awakens and nourishes in us our unsuspected inner powers.

The grand overview of Christian moral theology should be oriented to the primordial form of Jesus' announcement of salvation, as we find it in the beginning of Mark: "The time is fulfilled, and the kingdom of God has come near; repent, and believe in the good news" (1:14–15; see also Mt 4:12–17; Lk 6:14–15).

THE BASIC MODEL OF MORAL THEOLOGY

Christian moral theology and, needless to say, any corresponding moral pedagogy must remain true to this basic model. Those who preach salvation, those who attend to salvation by caring for others, and those to whom they speak must have an immediate sense that God sets us free for true life by the powerful gift of his love and grace. More than anything else, we want to be servants of joy. Then it will be evident that joy in God is our greatest source of strength.

The covenantal commandments, which we perceive in the light of the new covenant, and all specifically Christian norms can be seen as the expression of the all-embracing command to love God and our neighbor. They work together for the complete conversion both of the individual and the community, to the extent that we experience them as grace, as the Good News. And this kind of discourse about the covenant and grace, about the love of God, always takes precedence over any discourse about commandments.

This fundamental insight shaped the overall plan of my

moral theology, as I presented it to a broad reading public back in 1954 in my first major effort, *The Law of Christ*. Another decisive factor in my presentation was my deliberate decision to abandon the custom of the previous three centuries and *not* write a book of moral theology for the use of the priest in the confessional. My audience was and is meant to be all Christians who are concerned with being adult disciples of Christ. Here I was following the example of the great Johann Michael Sailer. More than a century before me he had published a splendid outline of a moral theology "for both laypeople and priests" that had found a lively echo among both Catholics and Protestants. But the Restoration that followed the Congress of Vienna blew a cold wind in his face and on his successful innovation.

Two hundred years before me, the founder of the Redemptorists, Saint Alphonsus Liguori (1696–1787), patron of confessors and moral theologians, had made an extremely important contribution to the renewal of moral theology. The discipline of moral theology in those days had reached a low watermark of legalistic rigorism. It remained mired in its focus as a model of morality for confessors.

Alphonsus's great achievement was to introduce a healthier view of the confessor's role. As opposed to the prevalent Western attitude of the confessor as judge, he borrowed the best features of Eastern Orthodox theology. The priest—especially in the confessional—is supposed to be a true image of the all-merciful Father. He is supposed to communicate the healing love of Jesus. And as for the "office of judge," the confessor should help people to understand the difference between authentic love and false mirror images.

A second merit of Saint Alphonsus is his idea of equiprobabilism, the consistent principle that the priest should not dare to impose burdens on anyone when either he or the penitent doubts that they are imposed by God. I have tried to maintain these two principles throughout my moral theology.

MORAL THEOLOGY FOR LAYPEOPLE

The audience for my teaching, as I have said before, was the adult Christian, that is, priests and laypeople on their way to becoming adult Christians. That choice of audience inevitably gives rise to a wholly different type of moral theology. It takes radical steps—steps that lead out of the sacristy and the confessional. It no longer deals just with "saving souls," but with saving the world, with training adult Christians who feel and demonstrate a sense of responsibility for the Church and the world.

Still, at this point, I would like to stress the fact that my position in no way meant that I had less esteem for the sacrament of reconciliation. I daresay that from my first years as a priest until my old age I was a much sought-after and prized confessor. Perhaps I may be allowed to illustrate this with an example. In 1968, I was invited by three Sicilian bishops to give a week-long course on the renewal of the sacrament of penance. We were also looking for new models of confession. Some time later, another bishop accused one of my hosts of having invited "this heretic," Bernard Häring, into his diocese. The bishop replied, "Why don't *you* invite him? Then you will see that all your priests are going to confession again. Father Häring had to spend half the night hearing confessions."

In my travels around the world, while giving courses on one subject or another, I have been invited by laypeople, as well as by priests, to celebrate with them the sacrament of reconciliation, both in public ceremonies and in private consultation. I hope the reader does not imagine that the reason for this phenomenon might be a certain amount of laxness on my part. A single example may erase that sort of suspicion. Once I was giving spiritual exercises for priests who, in keeping with the practice back then, were obliged to attend if they had let two years pass without making some sort of retreat. One priest I hadn't met came up to me and asked: "Should I even bother going to confession? I am a hopeless case. I've probably committed every kind of sin against the sixth commandment that could ever tempt anyone." "For my part," I replied, "there are no hopeless cases. We all live off God's goodness. But after you have told me your whole story, I will venture to invite you to start trying to become a holy priest. You will radically change your life only if you decide to." The priest made up his mind and accepted my words of encouragement. We kept in touch for a fairly long time, and I think I can say that he really did become a saint.

One more example: several people from a large parish told me, "We have had the good fortune to have a holy pastor." Years before this, I had had a similar conversation with this priest—the very same priest to whom they are referring: "You have only two choices," I told him, "either to strive resolutely for holiness or to become more and more a slave of sin." On such occasions, I would always remember how after my first Communion I had told my sister Konstantine: "I would like to become a saint." I'm a long way from that, but up until now I have stayed on the path, and I hope in the future to keep my eye fixed ever more firmly on the goal.

The Sacrament of Peace

In my writings, too, I have spoken out in various ways for the renewal and joyful celebration of the sacrament of reconciliation. For example, in the United States, my courses on confession led to a book titled *Shalom: Peace; The Sacrament of Reconciliation,* which became a religious bestseller and appeared in many translations. One English reviewer noted, "One hopes Father Häring hasn't come too late. If he had written this book ten years ago, we might have been spared the present crisis facing the sacrament of penance."

I have also directed a series of doctoral dissertations on the history of confession and current views about its renewal. Because of their relevance to this topic, I will mention here a few historical facts that are quite interesting from today's perspective. As late as the high Middle Ages, confessions made to laypeople were still highly valued. People liked to make their confession to monks who were not ordained. They were aware that wherever men and women admit their guilt and ask forgiveness, an act of grace occurs.

In Italy, for centuries abbesses had the authority to hear the confessions of their nuns and to absolve them. Again, for long centuries, at least before the Council of Trent, bishops and abbots gave general absolution in their parishes to all those present at communal confessions—with the sole exception that individuals who were aware of having committed serious sins had to confess them individually within a certain amount of time. The precise language used here is important: *"peccata gravia, et quidem criminalia"* ("serious and indeed *criminal* sins"). The sins for which forgiveness was withheld corresponded exactly to the ancient regulations for penance. They were all sins that were publicly known and the cause of serious scandal, in other words, "crimes." Centuries later—and this holds to our day—it became a strict obligation to confess all "serious sins" individually. This obligation led to the type of moral theology handbook that listed hundreds of "serious sins" and then had to cite the many criteria for clearly recognizing them. So, much that we have learned about the sacrament of reconciliation from past history points plainly to the future—a future that we have spoiled through our partial ignorance of the past.

Legal barriers that obscure the primacy of the gospels and grace have to be removed. In this respect, I think that through its careful study of history, the Academia Alfonsiana—not all by itself, of course—has made an important contribution to moral theology. I played a small part in this. The wall has now been breached; the primacy of grace in morality and pastoral care has won the day. However, there is no need to be surprised if transitions do not always come off easily and elegantly.

SERVING THE ETHICS OF PEACE

Serving the ethics of peace has always been an important dimension of my life's work, especially in regard to imitating the readiness to suffer of Jesus, the nonviolent Servant of God. Here I would simply like to go over a few aspects of my own evolution.

After my return from the Russian front, when it became especially clear to me that Divine Providence had called me to serve the renewal of moral theology, I was especially struck by the thought that service to peace had to become part of the core of Christian ethics.

Only after some years did I get a clearer realization that the whole issue of peace needed to be thought through and preached in the light of the healing power of nonviolence. The notion of a "love that ends all enmity" increasingly assumed a central position in this thinking. The love of his enemies that Jesus lived, that he died for, and that he preached is not some sort of love that keeps its distance. God loves us even when we were still enemies, says Scripture. A fully developed morality of faith and grace must clearly work out and organically incorporate the idea that active, creative, reconciling love always has to have priority. It is a key to the imitation of Christ as the peacemaker.

The love that ends enmity should not be limited to the individual person-to-person level, as indispensable as that may be. It has to become active, creative, and present at all levels. The commandment to make peace does not wait until war breaks out before it becomes an urgent mission. Christians have to be present at all levels and in all parts of the world as reconcilers, as enemies of enmity. They must learn the art of being everywhere, so as to form groups and communities that achieve competence in the art of ending enmity and that resist all shrinking back from sacrifice in action.

PEACE-KEEPING CENTERS

If we had encouraged and trained such centers and core groups among Christians in the former Yugoslavia, those outbreaks of ethnic madness that leave us speechless today would never have happened. I have nothing against the presence of U.N. peace-keeping troops. But the most pressing need of all is the contagious spread of the vocation to competence, or virtue, and the highest degree of skillfulness in ending enmity. That is a lot more than just disentangling a knot. It is the trick of getting people to "dovetail" in a way that sets them free. This holds true not just for Bosnia and the rest of the former Yugoslavia, not just for Rwanda and Burundi, Somalia and Cyprus, but in all parts of the world, at all schools, amid every kind of religious instruction, the splendid and urgent art of ending enmity must play a central role.

One can already cite some major steps forward. Many individuals, groups, and communities have realized that ecumenical conversion requires masterly action and self-sacrifice for peace and preservation of the creation entrusted to us, as well as the ecological virtues. But at the absolute center of all this is individual and community conversion to active nonviolence and the end of enmity.

These dimensions that I have outlined in this chapter are present only inchoately in my earlier work *The Law of Christ* (1954). By contrast, in my three-volume *Free and Faithful in Christ*, which I wrote during my fight against cancer and my confrontation with the Congregation for the Doctrine of the Faith (1977–1981), practically everything looks forward to the final chapter on peace and nonviolence. It is my hope that nonviolence, worldwide justice as an indispensable prerequisite for peace, and the noble and urgent vocation to ending enmity, will be the heart and soul of all moral theology in the future.

This message of peace and nonviolence is my legacy to my countless students and friends. Many people will have to sow and nurture this message in hopes of a rich harvest, indeed at times with the naked hope that the seed of humanity may not disappear from this planet. As I look back on my life, I only wish that I had managed better to introduce these concerns for an all-encompassing end to enmity and for active nonviolence into the whole of moral theology.

CHAPTER 6

THE CHALLENGE OF THE COUNCIL

A s with most of my contemporaries, the announcement
of a general council by Pope John XXIII came as a great
surprise to me. But I already knew that Pope John respected my work as I had outlined it in *The Law of Christ*,
so I was not surprised that, when the first appointments were
made, my name turned up as a consultant on the most important preparation commission, that on "faith and morals."
I was filled with high expectations. It was a good omen, I
thought, that when I walked for the first time down the Via
della Conciliazione, the wide avenue that leads up to St.
Peter's, on my way to work on the commission's business, I
ran into Father Henri De Lubac. We became friends, so to
speak, at first sight. Immediately afterward, we also met Yves
Congar; and the three of us usually sat together in the hall of
the commission.

The commission got down to work with a will. The
drawing-up of documents made rapid progress. But it soon
became clear that the majority of the members and consultants were rather conservative.

Right from the outset I was frequently in contact with
Bishop Joseph Schröffer from Eichstätt in Bavaria, later a
curial cardinal. I had a very special connection with the Ca-

nadian Cardinal Paul-Emile Léger and his compatriot Cardinal Maurice Roy. Professor Michael Schmaus, too, was an old acquaintance. Everyone was allowed to take the floor. By and large, an atmosphere of honest dialogue prevailed.

ON THE PREPARATORY COMMISSION

I was somewhat taken aback when I noticed that I had not been invited to join the two subcommissions that had to deal with moral issues. In these two subcommissions, two working papers were sketched out, one designated as *"De Ordine Morali"* ("On the Moral Order") and another on chastity, marriage, and the family.

However, when the texts came out in more or less finished form, I was enlisted, on orders from Pope John XXIII, to work with the subcommissions. Their moderator, Father Sebastian Tromp, S.J., gave me plenty of opportunities to take a position on the available texts. But the proposal on the moral order noted in advance that it was better not to talk about "love," because that word was open to misunderstanding. This statement was given in explanation of the use of the word "order." The text on chastity, marriage, and the family even argued that it was "forbidden to maintain that love is essential for marriage."

When he saw how disappointed I was, Father Tromp encouraged me to make a counterproposal. I wrote up an outline, which was destined to be incorporated into *Gaudium et Spes* in the section on the basic concerns of marriage. I was allowed to speak for about forty minutes. When I sat down, Father F. X. Hürth, S.J., (papal advisor to Pius XII on all moral questions and the editor in chief of the encyclical *Casti Connubii,* "On Christian Marriage," in which every attempt to impede the fertility of the marital act is characterized not just as immoral, but as a crime) answered in a very harsh and agitated tone, "This clearly contradicts the teaching of the Church." "If that's so," I said, "then I prefer to leave immediately."

But Father Tromp, who deep down probably shared Hürth's opinion, was a skilled and generally refined discussion leader, both in the commission and the subcommission meetings. He acted as mediator and said, though not in so many words, that in these meetings the commission members can and must have open discussion. And, indeed, this is what happened. Some members of the subcommission were obviously more inclined toward my point of view, and others were not.

When the long discussion was over, I helped Father Hürth (who was a physically broken, but who intellectually was a very vital old man) into his overcoat and held his hand as I guided him down the well-worn stairs of the Holy Office. Outside on the street, as I said good-bye to him, he looked very moved and said, "I hope you'll forgive my harsh words. Perhaps you can understand me better if I tell you that I argued for half a day on exactly this same point with Pius XI during the preparation of *Casti Connubii*. In the beginning he had expressed some ideas that your text vividly reminded me of." This remark was a hermeneutical key that helped me to understand better the whole text of *Casti Connubii*. From then on, Father Hürth was always friendly to me. Some time later, he lay deathly ill, and I paid him a visit that he seemed very grateful to receive. In the final years of his life, he seemed to have become a rather lonely man.

CONSERVATIVE VIEWS DOMINATE

As time went on, I presented the subcommission with quite a number of essential improvements for the existing drafts. A

Carmelite priest, who years later would become a cardinal, and who was obviously a very gifted man, gave me some friendly advice. "Father Häring," he said, "wouldn't it be better for the Council if you left the proposed text alone and simply distanced yourself from it? Despite your many individual improvements, the faulty basic structure remains, but then there's always the danger that the text will be passed." I also heard this sort of consideration from other friends who were working on matters for the general commission. But I stuck to my old, undiplomatic style and constantly tried to propose helpful improvements, even when I did not especially appreciate the text as a whole.

All in all, the atmosphere in the preparatory commission, including the subcommission, struck me as fairly amicable. I found the rather conservative bishops and consultants to be without exception honorable, upright men. Some, to be sure, came from a rather narrow ecclesiastical background and had a hard time understanding Pope John's efforts at *aggiornamento*, that is, interpreting the Gospel in such a way that by feeling our way into simultaneity with Jesus in his time we can better experience and preach Jesus in his simultaneity with us. *Aggiornamento*, the comprehensive inculturation of the Gospel with the highest degree of fidelity to the Gospel itself, moved forward with difficulty, though also at times with astonishing momentum. But the many documents that the various preparatory commissions had gotten ready for the printer months before the Council began were not, as yet, really encouraging.

A few months before the Council opened, Cardinal Julius Döpfner, Cardinal Bernard Alfrink, and Cardinal Leo Suenens asked me if I would, while on my many lecture tours, which seemed to deal almost exclusively with the Council, sound out people as to how far the texts of the preparatory commissions would be accepted or rejected by the Council. Shortly before the solemn opening of the Council, I told the three cardinals that, judging by everything I had heard or sniffed out, only the draft for the reform of the liturgy would pass; all the others would doubtless have to be thoroughly revised. "Father Häring," Cardinal Suenens remarked, "you've got an incurable case of optimism." After the Council, the same cardinal told me: "Well, everything went off far better than you dared to hope."

CHOOSING CANDIDATES FOR COMMISSION MEMBERSHIP

It was as clear as day that the results of the Council would largely depend upon the makeup of the conciliar commissions. For this reason Cardinal Achille Liénart of Lille and Cardinal Joseph Frings of Cologne told the assembled Council that they were against an immediate vote. One reason for this delay was that when the lists of candidates for commission membership had been drawn up, most of Council Fathers had not taken part in the process, and so we would first have to get to know one another. That same day Pope John's secretary Monsignor Loris Capovilla told me that the pope leaped for joy when the two cardinals' request was accepted with loud applause.

There followed hectic days of consultation as the lists were put together, and theologians who had collaborated on the Roman preparatory commissions were called in for advice. I was careful not to make suggestions of my own accord. But when I learned that the Italian bishops had split into three groups and hence were going to propose three different lists, I shared my concern with Cardinal Frings. If the Central European bishops did not include in their lists a few open-minded Italian bishops, the sad outcome might be that hardly any Italians would be elected to the commissions this time around. However, the Central European bishops did nominate some Italian bishops. And so, a whole series of outstanding Italian bishops was elected, especially those whom the Central European bishops conferences had put onto their common list. This act of open-mindedness greatly fostered a climate of collegiality among the various conferences of bishops.

Once again I found myself being called in. During the first sessions when Cardinal Giuseppe Siri publicly labeled the German bishops heretics, representatives of the Focolare Movement, an organization that is always concerned with peace-making, asked me to play mediator and arrange a dialogue between Cardinal Siri and the German bishops. Cardinal Döpfner, president of the German episcopate, immediately said yes. Despite persistent signals of friendship on my part, I got a harsh rebuff from Cardinal Siri. A later attempt in this direction was likewise rejected in a brutal letter to me. But this did no essential harm to the Council, since the great majority of the Italian bishops, who knew they were well represented on the commissions, were against any kind of faction-building.

The inaugural address by Pope John XXIII, which he wrote in his own hand, electrified the Council. I was moved and full of enthusiasm. Immediately afterward Cardinal Leon-Etienne Duval of Algiers asked me if I would address the French-speaking bishops about my reactions to this opening address. I did so in two back-to-back lectures, which the bishops urged me to publish. In very short order, I wrote the little book which in English is called *The Johnnine Council: Witness to Unity*. It first appeared in Italian, and Pope John XXIII was its first reader. He promptly sent Monsignor Loris Capovilla to me with a few presents—books from his own library.

As Capovilla later wrote, the pope noted in his diary that day: "I've just read Father Häring's book *The Johnnine Council: Witness to Unity* with great joy and complete agreement." He let me know that he felt fully understood.

WHIRLWIND OF COUNCIL WORK

During the four conciliar sessions, I was asked by many conferences of bishops from different language groups to lecture on the burning questions of the Council. To this day, I am amazed how I could do that, along with all the work of the commission, the editing, and so forth, and the many important discussions I was involved in, without destroying my health. Evidently, I am the type of person whose psychic state largely determines his physical condition.

After the end of the Council, while giving a course in the United States, I had heart trouble for the first time. The cardiologist to whom I was taken advised me to give up all my activities at once. My heart, he said, was quite overstrained and, most likely, incurably diseased. He prescribed strong medicines for me; and, when I asked how long I would have to take them, he replied with a serious look, "until your death." When I returned to Rome, a fellow Redemptorist recommended a highly regarded physician. This man drastically reduced the amount of drugs I was taking. He also said that I shouldn't give up my work but just allow myself more rest. My heart would soon calm down, he promised—and he was right.

INPUT TO *LUMEN GENTIUM*

I worked very intensively with the team drawing up *Lumen Gentium*, the great dogmatic constitution on the Church. I was assigned to do the final editing of Chapter Four, n. 30–38.

The text as I reworked it, following the commission's instructions, was accepted almost verbatim. This chapter dealt with laypeople in the Church. I also worked closely with the planning and execution of the chapter on the general vocation to holiness (*Lumen Gentium*, n. 39–42).

Both in my work on the commission and through lectures that I gave before entire conferences of bishops, I also fought energetically to save the text on "The Blessed Virgin and the Church" from becoming a separate constitution instead of the concluding chapter of *Lumen Gentium*.

Meanwhile, Cardinal Alfredo Ottaviani had spoken out decisively in favor of a separate constitution to treat the subject of our Lady. I was stunned when, after *Lumen Gentium* was passed, he told me, "On the question of where to put the statements on Mary, you were right. It was obviously the better solution." On the eve of the vote on the issue, I delivered a lecture-*cum*-discussion to the Redemptorist bishops, whom I managed to win over to my view. When the results were tallied, the votes of the Redemptorist bishops provided the margin of victory for the inclusion of the statements about Mary in *Lumen Gentium*.

QUASI-FATHER OF *GAUDIUM ET SPES*

My main contribution to the Council—at least when it comes to the amount of time and energy I put in—was in the pastoral constitution *Gaudium et Spes*. Cardinal Fernando Cento, the copresident of the mixed commission, to which this task was entrusted, publicly called me the "quasi-father of *Gaudium et Spes*." Of course, I consider this statement much exaggerated. On the other hand, I have to say that the constant support of this good-humored cardinal greatly encouraged me and my work.

I do not intend to write a commentary here on this extremely significant conciliar constitution, much less the whole story of its evolution. I am limiting myself, so far as possible, to my own role in it. I consider my work on *Gaudium et Spes* one of the high points of my life, and I thank God for the opportunity to make a contribution.

As early as the first conciliar session, Cardinal Leo Suenens and Giovanni Montini (later Pope Paul VI) proposed that the Council speak not only within the Church, but to the world outside, to the people of today's world. At first, the theological commission took on this assignment alone; then it was addressed by a large "mixed commission" of around thirty bishops and a similar number of *periti* (experts) from the theological commission, along with an equal group of coworkers from the conciliar commission for the laity. I was one of these many coworkers.

The work did not go smoothly. Influential forces on the theological commission tried to introduce the wretched preconciliar text "*De Ordine Morali.*" It looked completely out of place, and it did not have a trace of genuine dialogue with the world. Cardinal Leo Suenens, who belonged to the Council's central commission and was one of its moderators, called outstanding theologians such as Yves Congar and Karl Rahner to Mechlin in Belgium. The document they wrote was called simply the Mechlin draft.

On November 29, 1963, the assembly of the mixed commission, which now included a considerable group of laypeople (and even a few women) debated which of the two texts to choose. The discussion was long and passionate. Finally, I, too, was called upon to voice my opinion. I said that the Mechlin text was far preferable and gave it the praise it deserved. But, in my opinion, it was an excellent theological treatise for people trained in theology rather than the much-desired start of an authentic dialogue with people in the world of today.

At this point the session, which had long since worn all of us out, I was interrupted. I still recall that, during the pause, I had a long talk with a lay observer who agreed with my opinion. Then I went home, because I was very tired.

ON THE EDITORIAL COMMITTEE

I had barely arrived at the gate of our monastery on the Via Merulana when the brother on duty called me to the telephone. There was news from the commission. "The mixed commission has just now chosen an editorial committee. Bishop Emilio Guano of Livorno was named as its chairman. You were elected secretary. Do you accept the appointment? They are urgently asking you to say yes." It was not an easy choice for me. But the fact that a good man such as Bishop Guano had been elected chairman cheered me. He was surely one of the most erudite and sympathetic bishops I had ever met. Working with him was always a pleasure.

After a while, Bishop Guano and I joined forces on the same initiative. We proposed to Pope Paul VI that a number of bishops from the so-called Second and Third World be named as coworkers. Among the names we submitted was that of suffragan bishop Karol Wojtyla of Kracow, who in this way quickly became well known. With Guano's authorization, I also brought a group of outstanding women onto the mixed commission.

The other members of the editorial committee were monsignors Glorieux, Medina, Möller, and fathers Riedmatten, Sigmond, and Tucci, as well as two laymen, Professor Sugranyes de Franch and M. de Habicht. Together with Father Sigmond, O.P., and supported by his colleague Father

Dingemans from the Angelicum, we sketched out the first main section rather briskly. It bore the French title of "*La participation active de l'Église à la construction du monde,*" or, in English, "The Church's Active Participation in Building the World." It began with the words "*Gaudium et Luctus*": "The joy and grief of men and women today, especially of the poor and oppressed of every sort, are also the joy and hope, grief and mourning of the disciples of Christ." This programmatic text survived all reworkings. Then the text was strengthened, and the opening phrase now ran: *Gaudium et Spes*, or "joy and hope." It announced the subject and set the tone of the pastoral constitution. Until we finished working on it, I had the responsibility of translating the text into Latin and German, as well as of incorporating into it the concrete suggestions of the editorial committee— an overwhelming job.

Since time was pressing, Bishop Guano and the entire editorial committee gave me the task of working out the second and more concrete part of the text in a brief, tightened-up version. There was no longer enough time for thorough discussion in the whole mixed committee, so these chapters were called "annexa." The draft, which, for all the changes made in it, remained essentially intact, dealt with (1) promoting the dignity of marriage and the family; (2) the right way to support cultural progress; (3) economic life; (4) the life of the political community; and (5) the promotion of peace and building up the community of nations.

These annexes, separated from the full text of the first part, were delivered to all the Council Fathers in order to see which way the majority would go. It was clear to everyone that this presentation was only provisional. The complete text was the subject of lively discussion by the assembled Council from October 20 to November 5, 1964.

THE PINCERS OF THE PRESS

In the process I got caught up in an embarrassing situation, prompting Cardinal John Heenan, understandably enough, to rap me on the knuckles. Shortly before this session, the former bishop of Bombay, Thomas Roberts, S.J., had published an article in which he spoke to the Council about the population explosion. On the basis of his experience in India, he argued for greater openness toward married couples who, for reasons of conscience, had to limit the number of their children. The English episcopate issued an extremely harsh public reprimand to Roberts. At this point I got a call from a reporter on the staff of *The Manchester Guardian,* who asked me what I thought about the reprimand. I had already clearly presented to the commission behind closed doors the same case that Roberts made in public. I told my questioner more or less the following: The problem could not be so easily dismissed as the declaration by the English bishops might make it look. The journalist turned this exchange into an interview, which was not how *I* had seen it. But the worst thing was, indeed, that the paper printed the story on the first page with the large headline, "Father Häring Attacks English Bishops." My answer was in no way meant as an attack on the bishops of England.

In the council hall, Cardinal Heenan now shot vehemently back. One line from his speech became proverbial. Parodying a famous line from Virgil's *Aeneid,* he said, "*Timeo expertes et annexa ferentes,*" or "I fear the experts, even when they bear annexes." It was clear to all the Council Fathers that he meant me. The next day the archabbot of Beuron gave a humorous and skillful reply in my defense. I myself wrote immediately to Cardinal Heenan, apologized, and explained the mischief done by the journalist. Two days later, as I was walking down the Via della Conciliazione toward St. Peter's, I noticed Cardinal Heenan in full regalia only a few yards behind me.

Not until I came to the end of the street did I turn and wait for the cardinal. I introduced myself, but he promptly replied, "You don't need to tell me. The whole world knows Father Häring." I then asked whether he had gotten my letter of apology. He had just received it. We had a brief but very friendly conversation. Then, we walked together across St. Peter's Square, with the cardinal's arm around my neck. "Everybody," he told me, "has to see that we have reconciled." From then on, we were friends. Later on, Cardinal Heenan spoke out on the question of birth control along the same lines that I had done.

The episode with *The Manchester Guardian* and Cardinal Heenan's reaction had surely been noted in the Vatican. But I had no special problems as a result. Even *L'Osservatore Romano* was silent, although some time later, when a journalist from the Roman daily *Il Messagero* improvised an equally misleading "interview," *L'Osservatore Romano* launched a violent attack on me.

Around that time, there was a reorganization in the editorial commission that relieved me of some of the burden of my work. I remained the nominal editorial secretary, but Canon Hauptmann now took over the crucial work for the main part of the text. It did the cause good. On the subcommission for the chapter on marriage and the family in *Gaudium et Spes*, I was replaced by Father Edward Schillebeeckx, without being excluded from further collaboration. This reassignment, too, was a fortunate stroke of fate.

From start to finish, working along with others on *Gaudium et Spes* brought me into all sorts of contact with the non-Catholic observers at the Council. Among the many who made important contributions, I will mention only Lukas Fischer. Bishop Emilio Guano and I had long conversations with him.

Unfortunately, sickness forced Bishop Guano to leave before the conclusion of the Council's work. He was replaced by Cardinal Gabriel Garonne. Thanks, above all, to the powerful collaboration of G. Philips, everything finally came to a successful conclusion. After the next-to-the-last ballot, where the text as a whole was approved with more than a two-thirds majority, there were still twenty thousand "modi," or suggested improvements, to be dealt with, though, naturally, many of these were identical. I myself had once again become extremely active in formulating such "modi." I elaborated more than fifty, of which all but two or three were accepted. The primary reason for this work on the "modi" was that many of them were rather vaguely formulated. To clarify wording, with every suggestion for change, I offered a precisely worded version and explained specifically how it could be incorporated into the main text.

Among my suggested improvement some, I think, were extremely important. For example, together with my colleague Father Domenico Capone, I worked out new texts on the dignity of conscience so as to exclude language tainted with legalism. In this phase, of course, I could introduce my suggestions only by way of the Council Fathers who had the right to vote. I divided them up among a few friendly cardinals and the rest among Redemptorist bishops who shared my point of view on these issues. With regard to my suggestions on conscience, the commission agreed that it was good and much needed, but too long. Cardinal John Wright proposed leaving the job of shortening the draft to me—obviously he suspected that it came from me to begin with.

PAPAL INPUT TO *GAUDIUM ET SPES*

Last but not least, there was an unpleasant surprise. Paul VI sent in to the Council new, far-reaching, suggested changes. It wasn't clear whether or not they came from the pope himself or if he had just passed them on. They concerned article 51 in *Gaudium et Spes*, and in particular the problem of the morality of birth control. The pope's suggestions would have altered the text approved by the great majority of the Council Fathers into its exact opposite meaning. But, according to the conciliar rules decreed by the pope himself, this change was not permissible. I received the text late in the evening. Early the next morning, I woke up Cardinal Paul-Emile Léger and handed over to him my three-page answer, arguing that the commission was not allowed to accept the suggested changes sponsored by the pope. Then we both went to the plenary session of the commission, which had to be held precisely because of the pope's intervention. This session was a stormy one. The Dominican Cardinal Michael Browne said, "*Papa locutus est, causa finita,*" or "The pope has spoken, the matter is decided." The majority, however, were agreed that a *yes* to these new texts would throw the Council into a severe crises.

At this point, I quietly left the assembly room to see the papal deputy Angelo Dell'Acqua and ask for an audience with the pope. The Melkite archbishop Elias Zogby ran after me, grabbed me by the collar, and urged me, "Don't run away from your responsibility! Now we have to fight!" When I explained what I had in mind, he agreed with me. Since Dell'Acqua wasn't in his office at the secretariat of state, I waited patiently. Then, both Canadian cardinals, Paul-Emile Léger and Maurice Roy, came along unexpectedly. Roy had a text written by the laypeople at the Council. Cardinal Léger had my three pages. I bid farewell to them on the spot, glad that the two cardinals were taking up the burden of speaking frankly with the pope. That same day, the commission received the pope's answer, which made it clear that Pope Paul VI would absolutely respect the freedom of the Council.

In the following session that dealt with this issue, Cardinal John Francis Dearden of Detroit presided. All I can say is that he was simply tremendous. There was a new proposal concerning the text: the definitive decision on the question of birth control was to be left to the pope. This proposal became the famous footnote 14. It wasn't the best solution, but the best one possible under the circumstances.

That same evening, I was scheduled to give an interview on Italian television. It had been planned long before, in order to coincide with the end of the Council. The next morning's newspapers reacted to my TV appearance by saying that it obviously couldn't be true that the Council had been plunged into a crisis. Otherwise, Father Häring would not have been able to speak so calmly and confidently.

On December 6, 1965, the whole text was voted on. Of the Council Fathers, 1,309 voted *Yes*, and 75 voted *No*, and seven ballots were invalid.

WORKING ON THE DECREE ON PRIESTLY EDUCATION

I myself was never present at the meetings of the commission that was in charge of this matter. Every now and again I was consulted by commission members. After the next-to-the-last ballot on the text, I received a visit from the secretary of the commission, Father (later Cardinal) Augustin Mayer, O.S.B. He handed me a whole packet of proposed changes that had been submitted as *"juxta modum,"* or "qualified approvals" and that called for an outright condemnation of legalistic morality.

I looked these proposed changes over very closely and advised him that it was a bad idea to get involved with condemnations: first of all, because that was not the style of this Council; and second, because it would be a very complicated affair to say exactly what was or was not being condemned. After a little while, I handed Father Mayer the following suggested wording for note 16 of *Optatam Totius*:

> Likewise the theological disciplines must be restructured on the basis of the living contact with the mystery of Christ and salvation history. Special care is needed for the perfecting of moral theology. It must be nourished more richly from the teaching of Sacred Scripture. In its scholarly presentation, it must illuminate the loftiness of the vocation of believers in Christ and their obligation to bear fruit in love for the life of the world. Similarly, in the treatment of canon law and church history, the focus should be on the mystery of the Church in the light of *Lumen Gentium....*

The commission accepted my suggestion unchanged. But since it was a fairly long text, it had to be voted on separately. Only a few people voted no.

WORKING ON THE DECLARATION OF RELIGIOUS FREEDOM

I have a relatively modest part in the declaration on freedom of religion, *Dignitatis Humanae*. The first draft was worked out in Cardinal Augustin Bea's secretariat for ecumenism, mainly by Father John Courtney Murray, S.J., who for years had been the target of Cardinal Alfredo Ottaviani's Sacred Congregation of the Holy Office, now the Congregation for the Doctrine of the Faith. But the text also had to pass the commission for doctrine. A special subcommission was formed, and I was chosen as editorial secretary. We not only did not dilute the text; we strengthened its statements in several passages. But now Cardinal Ottaviani's technique of using adjournment as a delaying tactic set in. All our requests to discuss the document went for naught. We had to appeal to the pope, who ordered, in measured language, that the draft finally be discussed in the commission on faith and then passed onward.

For this important session, the bishops on the commission made a point of bringing in Murray. As chairman of the commission, Cardinal Ottaviani denied him the right to speak, noting that "there is too much freedom in the Church already." But since I had been elected editorial secretary for the document in question, the cardinal could not very well deny *me* the floor. I stood up and said, "Isn't it typical that you should be saying this? For many years, you have tried to gag Father Murray, and on this very same issue." The bishops applauded, and Ottaviani yielded.

John Courtney Murray took the floor and impressed everyone, first of all by the fact that—something scarcely expected from Americans—he spoke pure, polished Latin and, still more impressive was his imposing serenity. Even Ottaviani was visibly impressed. We got down to solid, objective work; and the decree managed to get passed by the Council in good time.

After that session, it happened that Cardinal Ottaviani and I were standing nose to nose in an overcrowded elevator. I broke the silence by saying, "Your Eminence, isn't it interesting that we find ourselves jammed so tightly together in the elevator. Don't we all live and think in the same tower, only while one of us looks out one window, the other looks out another?" My interlocutor immediately relaxed, and he answered amiably, "Oh, yes, dear Father Häring, that is how it is. And then, too, each of us wears a different pair of glasses and sees different colors." When we got to the ground floor, we stopped and had a conversation that lasted almost half an hour. The other commission members, who had witnessed our previous confrontation, were more than a little amazed. One supposedly said, "These two are either fools or saints."

I took part in Vatican II with my whole body and soul. No kind of toil was ever too much for me. In all the years after the Council, what counted most for me was to make it bear fruit everywhere. That was the point of my many working trips to Africa and Asia, and many other lands.

For me, as no doubt for many others, the Council was the great event of my life. It surpassed my most daring expectations. But even an optimist like myself could not fail to notice a series of compromises in the conciliar documents. Perhaps on a number of issues the great majority of the Council Fathers and the theologians working on the commissions let themselves be guided by the wish that practically all the Council's statements should win not just a large majority but something approaching unanimity. Still the optimist, however, I confidently hoped that the overall dynamic of the Council's results, in keeping with the convictions and goals of the great majority, would prevail. But we had underestimated the toughness of the minority—and a considerable portion of the laity. Ultimately, though, my basic feeling toward the Council is wonder, gratitude, and praise to God.

When I left St. Peter's after the Council's concluding ceremony, I happened to run into the two brothers from Taizé, Robert Schutz and Max Thurian. We exchanged heartfelt greetings, and I asked them whether or not they were satisfied with the outcome of the Council. "Satisfaction," they said, "would probably not be the full answer. We can only fall down, praise God, and adore the workings of the Holy Spirit." I think so, too.

CHAPTER 7

THE WATERSHED OF *HUMANAE VITAE*

M y optimistic view of the Church as renewed by the
Second Vatican Council continued unbroken until
1968. (Many people have told me they felt the same
way.) The issuing of the encyclical *Humanae Vitae,* or "Of
Human Life," which seemed to be concerned only with a
limited, specific problem, nevertheless hit the Church like a
late spring frost. At bottom, the issue at stake was a crucial
one that both the majority and the minority at the Council
had wrestled with mightily. This issue was one of collegiality
versus Roman centralism. At first glance, the problem was
how to find morally acceptable or tolerable methods of birth
control in an age when a rapid increase in world population
was unleashing violent social conflicts, endangering peace,
and threatening to upset the ecological balance of the whole
planet. But the core problem was how and by what authority were the appropriate moral norms to be determined.

A SUMMARY OF THE CHURCH'S ATTITUDE
TO BIRTH CONTROL

First of all, here is a brief history of the issue. In the first
centuries of the Church's existence, we find scarcely a trace

of comment on this problem. In any event, it had no central importance. To be sure, under the old Fathers and teachers of the Church, especially in the East, there were tendencies toward a certain sexual pessimism. But the dignity of marriage and the meaning of marital love, including sexual intercourse, were not as a whole in question. Influenced by a few Church Fathers, but above all thanks to the aftereffects of his Manichaean past, the great Augustine taught that marital relations were per se degrading, particularly when engaged in with passion. Intercourse was pardoned and rendered moral only by the express intention of creating new life. But this teaching scarcely affected the bulk of the laity or the pastoral care exercised by priests, since it was not a matter of Church discipline or public penance. Roughly speaking, we can say that up until a time after the Council of Trent, there was no general obligation to confess this "sin."

But beginning with the sixteenth century, all that began to change. Soon a rigoristic tendency came to the fore, vehemently insisting that any act of marital intercourse in which the transmission of life was impeded was a serious sin. Some rigorists held every sexual act to be sinful if it occurred at times or under circumstances in which conception was excluded. But this never became the common doctrine.

In the eighteenth century, Saint Alphonsus emphatically taught that the marital act is good in itself, as long as it is the expression of love and/or serves to promote fidelity. In his *Moral Theology*, Alphonsus wrote, "*Actus conjugalis est ex sese bonus, et hoc est de fide,*" or "The conjugal act is good in itself, and this is a matter of faith" (Book VI, treatise vi, n. 900). He added that the confessor should never initiate any discussion of the problem of *coitus interruptus*.

Into our century, most Catholic confessors have taken this advice. And as for those who did not, the faithful could easily avoid them. This relatively peaceful situation in pastoral care was altered at a stroke by the encyclical *Casti Connubii,* issued by Pope Pius XI in 1930. *Casti Connubii* was written primarily to counter a declaration by the Anglican Church on responsible parenthood that did not categorically exclude artificial methods of contraception. The preparation of *Casti Connubii* was a lonely, mountaintop decision—and here we touch on the key problem with *Humanae Vitae.* Two consultants to the Holy Office, Father F. X. Hürth, S.J., and Father Arthur Veermersch, S.J., actually wrote the text of *Casti Connubii.* Pius XI toned the text down by stressing the importance of married love. But deliberate contraception was nonetheless declared a crime (*crimen*).

I myself saw the catastrophic consequences of this at missions I preached in the years immediately after War World II. Hundreds of people came to me in confession after being denied absolution at an earlier mission in the 1930s for practicing contraception. They stood for hours outside my confessional once word had gotten around that Father Häring was very understanding on this critical point.

STUDY COMMISSION ON BIRTH CONTROL

During Vatican II, Pope Paul VI created a commission (Pontifical Study Commission on Family, Population, and Birth Problems) of recognized experts to study the question of birth control. Fewer than a third were theologians (that is, priests), the rest consisted of highly respected laypeople. At first, almost all the theologians were in favor of strictly condemning contraception, especially by artificial methods. Even among the laypeople, there were several individuals who had won a reputation for speaking out against contraception.

I, too, had been named to the commission by the pope.

But with me and with Auxiliary Bishop Joseph M. Reuss, the pope knew what he was getting: our positions on the issue were a matter of public record. Before the end of the Council, the members (primarily the theologians) on the papal commission met with the members of the conciliar subcommission (in connection with *Gaudium et Spes*). At the meeting, it became obvious that a clear majority favored the pope's lifting the sharp condemnation by *Casti Connubii*.

As for the members of the Council's subcommission on marriage and the family, I would like to add that as long as I served there as editorial secretary, I, together with Bishop Emiliano Guano, saw to it that a fresh group of bishops were continually being brought in. And these were men that we knew were convinced supporters of the doctrine expressed in *Casti Connubii*. But almost all of them changed their minds as soon as they were confronted with open discussion.

I have already pointed out that shortly before the end of the Council, the pope had reserved the question of contraception for himself. At that time, he likely had no idea that even a majority of "his" commission would come out for the lifting of the general ban on contraception. The commission did not come to its decision until sometime in the course of 1966 or 1967. Despite a gag order, the findings of the papal commission soon leaked out. The pope was much praised for not making such an important decision all alone in the Vatican, but for showing willingness to listen to the convictions of the whole people of God. I strictly observed the obligatory silence in everything related to my membership on the two commissions.

PAUL VI ISSUES *HUMANAE VITAE*

The news of the pope's decision to, in essence, support the restrictive norms of *Casti Connubii* struck us like a bolt of lightening. Who would have thought that Paul VI would go along with the views of a small minority? At the time I was involved with various activities in the United States, when journalists from the *New York Times* and *Life* magazine came calling. They showed me the text of *Humanae Vitae*. I was full of consternation and asked from what source had they gotten the text. When they asked me for an interview on the encyclical, I inquired once again about the source of their information. "It only cost us $1,000," they crowed. I rejected their demand, which would have been a sinful act of collaborating with this violation of the oath of secrecy.

Since I could foresee that as soon as the encyclical was published, I would be besieged by a flood of questions, I withdrew into a convent of nuns in Santa Clara, California. I gave out my address only to my superiors. So I was all the more flabbergasted when suddenly the phone began ringing day and night. Respected theologians, marriage counselors and many others called up to find out what I thought. At first I refused to answer. But when one theologian told me that he was going to leave the Church, I chided him and began to pray to learn what God's will for me might be. Soon I heard from doctors in California that some of them had already announced their intention of leaving the Church. Now the question I asked myself before God was this: *Would I be able to handle all the troublesome consequences of taking a public stand?* I did not decide until I read that Cardinal Angelo Felici was quoted in *L'Osservatore Romano* as saying that "whoever is unwilling to accept the norm of *Humanae Vitae* should leave the Church."

SPEAKING OUT AND ITS AFTERMATH

Come what might, I had to do everything I could, in conjunction with others, to prevent a gigantic wave of departures from the Church. I gave a brief interview to the *New York Times*, with remarks that boiled down to this: All Catholics have to sincerely examine themselves in the eyes of God to see whether they can in conscience agree with the norm of *Humanae Vitae*. If they can, then they have to make every effort to translate their yes into actions. Those who after thorough reflection before God *cannot* convince themselves that the norm is correct and livable should follow the sincere findings of their conscience. But that decision was no way a reason for leaving the Church.

Then I headed to Rome so that in the following weeks I could give courses I had promised for priests and bishops in Sicily. I met the general of my order, the Very Reverend Tarcisio Amaral, a Brazilian. I had already informed him about my painful decision; so I was more than a little surprised when he said nothing to me about the matter. Only after I returned from giving my two courses did he call me in for a discussion. He told me that shortly after my interview he was summoned by the cardinal secretary of state, Amleto Cicognani, and asked to use his influence to get me to retract my statement. He answered: "On this question Father Häring is no doubt more competent than I am. However I will invite him to report to me, as soon as I have a chance." Evidently, he didn't want to upset me before I left for Sicily and Sardinia.

Immediately after my return, Father General set a date for me to talk with Cardinal Cicognani. I was called in immediately. The cardinal had already been precisely informed by the Canadian papal nuncio Emanuele Clarizio. While I was in the United States, Monsignor Clarizio had invited me to come speak to him about this issue. Evidently no one had considered having me get together with Cardinal Egidio Vagnozzi, the apostolic delegate in the U.S., because it was known how often he had come out against me. The conversation with the nuncio in Canada was wide-ranging. And I saw, too, that accurate information about this matter had indeed been transmitted to Cardinal Cicognani, who, when I met him, treated me in as refined a fashion as had Monsignor Clarizio.

For as long as Cicognani was secretary of state, I never had any serious problems with the Vatican. And I had a loyal friend in the person of the longtime Sostituto, Angelo Dell'Acqua in the secretariat, a man I could turn to at any time. Perhaps I owe it to him that in the *Humanae Vitae* affair I was handled as gently as I was. Dell'Acqua later was the papal vicar for the diocese of Rome. On the day that he died, in Fátima, he ordered the priest who was accompanying him to pay me a personal visit and to express his thanks to me for all my pastoral work in Rome. He especially wanted to thank me for the loving care I gave priests who were going through crises. It was good for me to know that I had friends in the Vatican who could put in a word for me and who, when it was needed, were glad to do so.

QUESTIONS OF CONSCIENCE

Back in 1968, acting from purely pastoral motives, I wrote several articles on the questions of conscience raised by *Humanae Vitae*. These questions were putting many Catholics to a severe test. The most widely read article was the one published in *Commonweal*. I sent practically the same text, but in German, to Cardinal Julius Döpfner, archbishop of Munich-Freising. As he was away at that time, his deputy had the essay printed in the *Münchener Kirchenzeitung*; and it was reprinted elsewhere. It anticipated more or less everything that the Königstein Declaration, a pastoral statement on the encyclical issued by the bishops of West Germany, suggested by way of pastoral relief. Before I flew back from North America, I was called in to consult with a number of American and Canadian bishops. Neither we theologians nor the many bishops conferences, which through their official declarations, offered help to people in reaching and respecting a conscientious decision, were directly looking to dissent from the encyclical's teaching as such. Still, I never shut myself off from the efforts of hundreds of moral and pastoral theologians who expressly asked the magisterium to rethink collegially or revise its insistence on the essential sinfulness of contraception.

On the papal commission that preceded *Humanae Vitae*, minority representatives had argued primarily that the papal teaching authority, above all on questions of sexual ethics, might suffer great harm if a teaching so heavily stressed as the one in *Casti Connubii* were to be officially revoked. I countered that the Petrine service of the pope within the Catholic Church and with regard to ecumenism would in the long run gain a lot of prestige, if the pope, after mature reflection, were to declare that a given nonrevealed teaching could be thoroughly modified.

Had the pope asked my advice, it would have run along these lines: he ought to publish the position taken by the great majority of his commission along with that of the minority. And, I thought, he should clearly state that he personally agreed with the minority theologians. But the conscience and convictions of those who sided with the majority on the commission absolutely had to be respected in the Church. Paul VI showed his human greatness by the fact that he did not contradict the many dissenting public statements (such as the Königstein declaration) by the large conferences of bishops, and in fact showed respect for them.

It is well known that, before the publication of *Humanae Vitae,* the later John Paul I shared the opinion of the majority on the commission. But after the publication of the encyclical, he cautiously spoke out for accepting it. As pope, he immediately began to worry about finding a more harmonious solution. By contrast, Karol Wojtyla was definitively one of the people who had advised Paul VI to follow the direction he did in his encyclical. The patient working out of all the old and new problems of sexual ethics is unthinkable without collegiality. No other problem makes it so evident that rigid centralism is of no use when it comes to an idea so pregnant with life as inculturation or the reappraisal of the past. We can readily predict that in the future, the Council's initial efforts on collegiality will fully expand. But for many people the transition has been and will be a painful one.

CHAPTER 8

EXPANDING HORIZONS

From my childhood as a farm boy in a small mountain village, to the international forum of Vatican II in Rome, to worldwide teaching venues, my life has been a journey of gradually expanding horizons and responsibilities. Divine Providence took me out of the narrow confines of a peasant village and led me far away. I remember well the powerful advance of trust given to my boyhood friend Hannes and me when we were allowed to take the two-day trip to Gars to enter the Redemptorist *Progymnasium*. It was a new world.

And when Hannes and I attended the public *Gymnasium* in Günzburg while boarding at the Alphonsianum, we found another new world. Even though we boarded at the Redemptorist Alphonsianum, I still had connections with the outside world. And I soon learned how small the world is. On the way home from school, a farmer's wife, who was returning from market, called out to me and said: "It's written all over your face: you must belong to Franzili Häring in Böttingen. Your face could be a carved image of your mother's."

Even as I entered the confined milieu of the novitiate, I never had the feeling of being penned up. On the contrary, I discovered the deep and broad horizon of spiritual life, thanks to an excellent library and a novice master who knew all

---

about life. The path into the depths makes possible a healthy journey into the distance.

FROM A SMALL WORLD TO BROADER VISTAS

The next broad vistas that opened to me were through my studies at the Redemptorist college, which was located at first in Rothenfeld near Andechs, then, after the Nazis confiscated the Rothenfeld property, in Gars. There a whole group of professors, above all, Fathers Viktor Schurr (dogmatic theology), Alois Guggenberger (philosophy) and Englebert Zettl (church history) enabled the valuable expansion of my spiritual horizon. These new vistas were something for which I was always looking.

Out of the protected but not cramped environment of the monastery, I was then hurled overnight into the barracks and out to the front lines of World War II. The many and various friendships, some of them quite close, that I had with men from utterly different backgrounds once more gave me fresh opportunities to broaden my horizon.

After a brief training as a medical orderly in Munich, my unit was assigned to Ebingen, which was home ground. Above all, I enjoyed speaking my beloved Alemannic dialect once more with my "house people"—my cordial hosts. Every new, warm human connection, whether it was with soldiers or civilians, Germans, Frenchmen, Poles, Ukrainians, or Russians, offered hitherto unknown perspectives. This was especially true when it was not a matter of superficial relationships, but of comradeship or friendship at times when the question really was "To be or not to be." I returned home in 1945, a mature and experienced man.

I do not want to forget the broadening of my Catholic horizon in the direction of the ecumene. I am thinking, for example, of my French comrades, who, when I was posted to France, asked me to hold regular Bible study sessions in the evening. Through friendship with men and women of different persuasions my understanding of my own Catholicism became more profound and extensive. When I remember all this, I can only say how very grateful I am to Divine Providence.

The year and a half I spent in Tübingen offered still another kind of expansion. As a student of both the best Protestant and Catholic professors, and as someone who was on friendly terms with a number of them, I began for the first time to get a full sense of how my life history could give me the gift of an ecumenical vocation. Another contributing factor here was the subject proposed by Professor Theodor Steinbüchl for my doctoral thesis: "The Holy and the Good: The Reciprocal Relationship Between Religion and Morality."

PASTOR TO REFUGEES

While I was in Tübingen, at the request of the diocesan authorities, I looked after the groups of Catholic refugees that were just then beginning to form into parishes. Every Sunday I gave religious instruction for adults and children, and celebrated Mass in two different places. I found that this in no way distracted me from work on my doctorate. Theology has to be lived, above all, in its pastoral dimension.

Immediately after getting my degree in June 1947, I began to teach moral theology and the sociology of religion at the Redemptorist college in Gars. It was fortunate that almost all my students brought with them experiences from the war and, in some cases, from Russian POW camps. Our work together was mutually enriching, a continuous departure toward new horizons. And then there was the lively dialogue I had with my highly qualified colleagues.

With an occasional interruption, I taught at least one semester every year in Gars until 1958. Thereafter, I went to Gars only in passing to give brief courses.

During those years, I was often involved with pastoral care by helping out in parishes on weekends. I helped prepare regional missions through my research on the sociology of religion and pastoral exercises for the clergy of these regions. On some occasions, I also participated directly in the mission in one parish or another.

Still, the work that probably counted most for myself and my long-term responsibilities was the so-called refugee missions. Together with Father Spielbauer, an experienced giver of missions, and Father Viktor Schurr, we three started a program that was later joined by several dozen missioners. The first attempt was in the region of Coburg that once had been exclusively Protestant. Sometime before we arrived, Father Spielbauer traveled to all the places we were to visit on our mission in order to find lay assistants and win them over to the cause. Each one of us had to cover a whole host of villages and little towns where there was no organized pastoral care for Catholic refugees. We were absolute pioneers and sometimes had to improvise. The lay assistants gave us the addresses of Catholics, every one of them a refugee. We usually said Mass in a rented dance hall or a some such other similar locale.

ON MANY FRONTS

This work made it plain to me that before you can preach you must first listen lovingly to what your audience has to say. I delivered none of the model sermons I had carefully prepared; instead, I grappled with people's distress, their worries, fears, and hopes. Looking back, it strikes me as miraculous how quickly new communities took shape. Every year, I returned to the Coburg-Ansbach area for around ten weeks, usually on my vacation.

These years saw the creation of my three-volume work *The Law of Christ*. Without the widening of my horizons through exploratory pastoral care and the many joyful and serious experiences it brought, my work would have turned out quite differently.

During the years in Gars, I accepted the invitation of the recently founded International Catechetical Institute in Brussels and, over a period of eight years, I gave a course comprising about thirty lectures (in French). My audience was made up, not of young people, but of men and women from all over the world who already had or were designated for responsible jobs in religious education. Here, too, dialogue and readiness to listen were the keys to expanding my view of the world.

But my great opportunity was the call to the newly established Academia Alfonsiana in Rome with its explicit goal of working together for the renewal of Catholic moral theology on the foundation of Holy Scripture, Christian tradition, and the social sciences. The start-up could succeed only through the generous cultivation of dialogue among the professors and with the students, many of whom already brought with them a rich experience of life and pastoral care. As I look back on almost fifty years there, I think I can say that the Academia Alfonsiana has distinguished itself through the depth and breadth of its Catholicity. It has also never neglected the ecumenical dimension.

Upon the spontaneous recommendation of Dr. Douglas Steere, the Quaker observer at the Second Vatican Council, I was invited over a period of years by the very active ecumenical group that called itself the Church of the Savior to preach spiritual exercises in their retreat house at Dayspring. Each time, they were an enriching and happy experience for me.

TIMES OF JOY

One joyful high point of my life was the two weeks that I spent in Dunblane with the leading men and women of the Church of Scotland, one of the Reformed Churches that originated with John Calvin. The Church of Scotland has an unusually strong ecumenical thrust and is well informed about ecumenism. During the first eight days, I went very early in the morning to the Catholic church where I concelebrated the Eucharist.

On the ninth day, I could immediately sense a special atmosphere of expectation or rather of solemnity. The head of the Church of Scotland, Dr. Jan Frazer, asked me, in the name of the whole group, to share with them a one-time eucharistic hospitality. I was completely surprised and said something like, "I'm thinking now about the fact that even the Anglican Church has so far refused eucharistic community with you. Pardon me, I feel momentarily confused." At which point, their leading theologian said, "Father Häring, did we hear you right?" I could only say a firm yes. Then this pious theologian proposed, "Let's just all say one after another what the Lord's Supper means to us." I could not get over my astonishment at the depths of piety and theological competence from which all of these testimonies to faith arose. In the end, the theologian made his profession of faith in this way, "On the cross Jesus wasn't just hanging there. He was all there, wholly present in totally self-donating love for us.

In the Eucharist the same Lord is pure presence and gift for us." All those present said a loud and joyful *Amen.*

Later, Dr. Frazer wrote, "Then Father Häring spread out his arms and beamed at the words 'What's stopping us?'" On the final day of our course, we all went together to the Catholic church in Dunblane, whose pastor had agreed to be our host. I was the celebrant. After the first reading, the chief theologian from the Church of Scotland delivered a brief but gripping address. After the Gospel, I gave a homily about the Eucharist as the great sign of unity and reconciliation. The first ones to come to communion were Dr. Frazer, then the well-known theologian, and then everyone else. There were just enough consecrated hosts to go around. The further dialogue on the day we said good-bye was like reliving the events in the hall where we celebrated the Eucharist.

Naturally, the Catholic bishops of Scotland heard all about this. Out of politeness, I had informed them about the invitation from the Church of Scotland, and they were certainly glad to hear about it. But on the subject of sharing the Eucharist with Protestants, they observed, "Father Häring has a good heart, but sometimes he is not very prudent." There is probably nothing that made the horizon of Christian unity more clearly perceptible than those memorable two weeks in Dunblane.

Incidentally, during that trip I found in the old library of the Church of Scotland a Latin translation of the Qur'an by the monks of St. Bernard, with a foreword by Martin Luther that was far from flattering for those who venerate Islam's holy book.

From time to time I sent information about my ecumenical activities to the Pontifical Council for Promoting Christian Unity (formerly the Secretariat for Promoting Christian Unity), which has been in operation since the Council, or consulted with it for approval of invitations. They gave me nothing but encouragement.

Before the Council, my activity had already taken on a European dimension. I gave lectures and courses in many cities of Italy, in France, Belgium, Holland, England, Ireland, and Spain. With the Council, my horizon expanded by meeting bishops, theologians, and laypeople from every continent. After the Council, I spent my long academic vacations and free semesters in Africa, Asia, and in North and South America.

DIALOGUE WITH AFRICAN NATIONS

The invitations followed from the episcopates, bishops conferences, pastoral institutes, and missionary orders. I described my "vacation" activities in Africa in my book *I Have Learned With Open Eyes*, which was translated into Swahili, by now the most widespread written language in Africa.

In these varied labors, I have prized dialogue above all things. I wanted to learn where the different peoples and tribes of Africa and Asia stood vis-à-vis receiving the Good News of the Gospel in their hearts. Were they trying to incorporate it creatively into their history, to inculturate it into their life? We have no right to impose the Gospel on Africans, Asians, and so on, in the guise of European conceptual schemes and ways of thinking. All my work and my encounters in these cultures, which at first struck me—and many other Westerners—as so alien, widened my horizon and allowed me to better understand the originality and universality of the Gospel.

I was active in the following countries of Africa: Kenya, Tanzania, Uganda, Malawi, Zambia, Zimbabwe, South Africa, Lesotho, Burundi, Rwanda, Zaire, Cameroon, Nigeria,

Chad, Niger, Togo, and Ivory Coast. If the African peoples are given their full freedom, if they are not prevented from developing their own traditions, they will bring in a priceless treasure for the world and for the Church.

The festivals that I was allowed to join in while I was in Africa, their way of singing the Gospel, opened up to me new dimensions of the experience of faith. The Africans I met sensed how much I respected and loved them. And they returned this gift of love a thousand times over. Two otherwise insignificant episodes should make this clear. In 1977, after my third operation for cancer, I was at death's door. The doctors themselves proclaimed that "Father Häring is on his deathbed." Some of the African media picked up this report, and the archbishop of Bujumbura in Burundi, Michael Ntuyahaga, held a solemn, well-attended requiem Mass for me in his cathedral. Afterward, as a matter of course, my name was entered into the list of ancestors, and there was a dance for these ancestors. Later at a conference in Europe, an African woman theologian elegantly performed the dance of the ancestors for me. I think I can be sure that when I die, people will remember me in many places.

The second episode that shows how close my heart is to the peoples of Africa occurred on the occasion of my golden anniversary as a priest. Bishop Peter Kwasi Sarpong, then president of the Theological Union of Africa, delivered the festive sermon and lecture in my home parish, much to the astonishment of my compatriots.

SPIRITUAL WORK IN ASIA

I gave courses in the following countries of Asia: Israel, India, Indonesia, Malaysia, Singapore, the Philippines, Korea, Hong Kong, and Japan. In India and the Philippines, they let me lead spiritual exercises for the bishops. I was deeply impressed.

In the Philippines, there was an explosive tug of war among the bishops that came to a resolution while I was present. The president of the conference of bishops had invited me to lead spiritual exercises for the group. My arrival had ignited a rift among the bishops. A year before, the famous American TV-bishop, Fulton Sheen, had preached a retreat to the bishops. He came with his secretary, flying first class. (His traveling expenses were paid by the Filipinos, naturally.) But when Bishop Sheen vehemently admonished them to back Ferdinand Marcos in his struggle with the Communists, he so irritated the younger bishops, and even some of the older ones, that they left before the exercises were over.

My job, and it was no easy one, was to reconcile the warring factions. Every evening the younger bishops, in addition to the day's three lectures, held an hour for reflection and prayer. Finally, they were ready to approach the other group, which hitherto had sworn to stand by Marcos. Ultimately, the president of the conference of bishops expressed his thanks from the altar, and added as his final words: "We were told by the Redemptorists that when Father Häring is in the Third World, he is not allowed to accept an honorarium, reimbursement for traveling expenses, or even any gift of value. But we have to give him some present, and our gift is this: the unanimous promise that we will stand on the side of the poor and the political prisoners, committing ourselves to nonviolent action for change." A check for a million dollars would have been dirt compared with this pledge.

My friends Jean and Hildegard Goss-Meier immediately came over and gave a series of courses and training sessions on nonviolence. We praised God when the nonviolent transfer of power from Marcos to Corazón Aquino took place.

In the courses I gave in Indonesia, I made the astonishing discovery that of the eight moral theologians active in the country seven had studied at the Academia Alfonsiana, and the eighth had introduced my *Law of Christ* as his textbook.

In Thailand, the bishops and even the nuncio participated in the courses. At the conclusion, we had a concelebrated Mass in Bangkok. Despite my protests, I was compelled to be the main celebrant, with the nuncio, the bishops, and priests joining in.

The courses in Korea were mobbed, with many laypeople in the audience. And I also got a pleasant surprise there: I had been asked to make the drafts of my lectures available two months before I was scheduled to give them. When I arrived, they handed me a thick book in which the lectures had already been printed in Korean. A copy was given to all participants. As a result, I never actually gave the lectures, and we had a very lively discussion instead.

The three weeks in Hong Kong were highly satisfying, too. The first thing I should mention is the wonderful Chinese hospitality. The bishop had done an excellent job of making all the preparations. Eight evenings were reserved for the young people, with a different topic for each evening. The first one was "Prayer—Gaining the Center." It was very well attended, with non-Christians as well as Christians among the audience. My greatest surprise was that at the end of the evening, the young people asked me to continue dealing with the subject of prayer on the next evening. This time the hall could not hold the crowd, and many people had to sit on the floor. Once again, there was a general request to stick with the subject of prayer. For myself, and no doubt for my listeners, this week was a true feast.

I went to Japan twice. For the first trip, my superiors

had wanted me to give a retreat for my German fellow Redemptorists. But one hundred and fifty participants showed up, and I had to preach in English. The atmosphere was extremely cordial. As usual, I did not bring much luggage for the long trip, and I always washed my clothes myself. But in Japan I went to a store in the very first week to buy some new shirts. I didn't want to stick out among so many neatly dressed people. In Japan, everything was so thoroughly organized that in a month I gave one hundred lectures, in different languages, sometimes with simultaneous translation.

ON THE ROAD IN SOUTH AND NORTH AMERICA

From Japan, I flew via Central America to Brazil, where I likewise did a stint of a hundred lectures, plus a few interviews and talks on TV. In Mexico as well, I gave three weeks' worth of lectures.

One of my last long trips was to participate in the congress of Latin American moral theologians in São Paulo. Cardinal Paulo Arns greeted the heavily attended conference; and I had the honor of delivering the opening lecture. I spoke about the therapeutic, reconciling dimension of liberation theology from the standpoint of Christian ethics. I was more than sightly amazed to see that almost all the moral theologians of Latin America considered themselves my "disciples."

The circuit of my apostolate widened more than geographically. Quite unaware, I fell into the world of the mass media. Above all in the United States, I would frequently be invited to speak on radio or TV, and the same requests would occur in Italy. There I also began a regular collaboration with *Famiglia Cristiana*, the magazine with by far the widest circulation in the country. Every week for around fifteen years I published in it a brief essay and/or an answer to a reader's letter. Every year, a thousand or more readers wrote to me; a secretary on the editorial staff selected the most relevant questions. One estimate by the editors, based on a poll, claimed that five to seven million Italians regularly read my piece. Wherever I turned up in Italy, whether on trains or the boat to Sardinia, perfect strangers used to greet me with, "Hello, Padre Häring."

Since some of my contributions on questions about family life had evidently met with some interest, the staff of RAI (the Italian Broadcasting Corporation) called upon me for continuous collaboration on the subject of family life. The network policy of "equal time" suggested that alongside a priest-commentator there had to be a Communist from the commission on the family. Seldom have I have found anyone so easy to work with as this so-called Communist. He backed all or almost all of my suggestions.

Neither I nor my friends can figure out how a little farm boy from a remote mountain village could end up speaking to so many people. I wrote in German, Italian, English, and sometimes in French around ninety books, including my works on moral theology: *The Law of Christ* (1954) and *Free and Faithful in Christ* (1978-1981). The ninety books went through about three hundred translations into many languages. Insofar as they served the Gospel and human civilization, I can only thank Divine Providence for the opportunity to write them. It is a special joy to me that my postconciliar Chinese-language edition of *The Law of Christ*—with the permission of the central government—was allowed to serve in many Chinese seminaries as a textbook, as it still does. The only way I can explain the granting of permission is that on the topic of inculturation, I stressed how senseless it was to import the Stoic, Greek, or any other ancient European teaching about virtue, into high Chinese culture. After all, the Taoist or Confucian teaching on virtue is far more noble and more closely approximates the biblical perspective.

CHAPTER 9

HOUSES OF PRAYER

—————

S ome years ago, the generalate of the Trappists in Rome
sent a few of their monks to the Academia Alfonsiana.
They were obviously quite satisfied with their educational
experience there, and told their superiors so. Thus it came
about that the generalate invited me to preach a retreat for
the brethren of the generalate. There followed invitations from
the abbey of Mount St. Bernard in England, from an abbot
in America who had been a Redemptorist and my superior
at the Academia Alfonsiana, and from the abbey of Geth-
semani, home of Thomas Merton, with whom I also had a
very fruitful encounter.

In exchange for these retreat sermons among the
Trappists, I had requested the favor of sharing their common
life for a while. I was so taken with these experiences that,
after mature reflection, I asked the general of my order, the
Very Reverend William Gaudreau, to let me transfer to the
Trappists.

But my request left him rather vexed. "Up till now," he
said, "whenever I have gotten requests like this, I have given
an enthusiastic yes. With you, it is different. You must not
run away from the responsibility that has accrued to you in
the Church." And he stood his ground. Ultimately, I saw in

—
131

this a sign of God's will. In this searching for God's will for me, I obviously I had to think over the question of what renewal of prayer life meant for me, as well as what it meant for orders and congregations that are mainly dedicated to the apostolate or education.

TRAINING IN PRAYER

From 1962 on, I was contacted by nuns from various active congregations, most especially the nuns from the motherhouse of the Sisters of the Immaculate Heart of Mary (IHM) in Monroe, Michigan. They were founded by a Redemptorist who later became a Trappist. They approached me with a question that I myself had already discussed with Thomas Merton and others: What role does continuous training in prayer play in orders and congregations devoted to the apostolate and charitable activities?

In 1965, this circle and I got together to make a concrete proposal to the annual conference of women superiors in America: that every active congregation choose at least one of their houses where the whole rhythm of life would be governed not directly by the apostolate but by the tireless practice, and the constant learning, of prayer. They could be called simply "houses of prayer," with a view to Isaiah 56:7: "These I will bring to my holy mountain, and make them joyful in my house of prayer."

In June of 1966, I was asked to preach spiritual exercises for the general chapter of the IHM sisters in Monroe. This time I went into more detail on the idea of making "a house of prayer in every congregation," not in addition to the other houses, but as a model for constant learning, for prayer as the real center of life both of the individual and of the community. The response of the sisters to this suggestion was very lively, and they seriously discussed every aspect of it.

I was overjoyed when soon afterward I was informed by telephone that the general chapter had unanimously accepted my proposal. The superior general, Sister Margaret Brennan, was qualified in every way to turn the plan into reality. The supreme goal was that the house of prayer would serve the whole congregation as a school for prayer, so it could renew itself in the spirit of the Second Vatican Council.

The sisters were practical in designing their plan. They consulted Thomas Merton shortly before his death. He, too, was enthusiastic about the idea of a house of prayer. In the following years, well-prepared conference meetings took place in Monroe. During six weeks, one hundred and thirty-seven nuns from nineteen different congregations participated. Breaking up into fourteen groups, or houses, they experimented practically, intensively, and enthusiastically; and I myself joined in. The interest and excitement for this task could not have been greater. Both the participants and I spread the good news everywhere; and I did not hesitate to spread the word about this decision wherever in the world I went traveling. By 1967 we had made a detailed presentation of the concept in the journal *Review for Religious*.

CREATING HOUSES OF PRAYER

In Monroe, these early years of enthusiasm saw the creation of a house of prayer on some farmland that belonged to the motherhouse. On this land was an abandoned farmhouse whose barn was very nicely rebuilt into a prayer center. The prayer center included a guest room that I was often allowed to use. We were quite surprised when in the Monroe town archives, someone found the old deed of gift to the church from the indigenous landowner who had been born on that property. The place on which the house of prayer stood, and the land around it, was offered in dedication by the owner with the remark that "it may become for all times a house of prayer."

Along with the superior general, Margaret Brennan, who is also an outstanding theologian, let me also mention the nuns who led the way in translating the idea into a reality: (1) Sister Mary McDevitt, who became the superior of the first house of prayer in Monroe and who was the directress of the whole continuing education program for her congregation; (2) Sister Mary Jo Maher, who creatively spread the idea first in Brazil, and then all over Latin America, combining, in a unique way, deep charisma and charm; (3) Let me further mention with great gratitude Sister Ann E. Chester. From the very beginning, she was there with heart and soul and a great deal of initiative. She turned the spacious Kresge House in Detroit into a much-visited and admired school of prayer for many people. She probably contributed more than anyone else to the worldwide spread of this initiative. From the outset to this day, the Kresge House has been an optimally functioning information center for everything that has to do with the plan for houses of prayer.

The sisters involved in the first prayer house, significantly named Visitation House, were responsible for, among other things, the founding of two houses of prayer in Africa. Visitation House, with its attractive barn-church, likewise became in the course of time a visitors' center. There, following the example of Mary, Elizabeth, and Zechariah, many people came together to blend their voices in praising God and to dedicate themselves to the apostolate of prayer. The barn-church soon became the site of an extensive lending library with books on every dimension of prayer, freely available to every visitor.

I myself feel obliged in many ways to thank heartily the IHM sisters, and, above all, those who made Visitation House into an attractive center for the apostolate of prayer and the prayer school. Whenever I could spend one or two weeks with them, my heart was increasingly caught up in Elizabeth's praise of Mary, in Mary's *Magnificat*, Zechariah's *Benedictus*, and the leaping for joy in the womb of the baby John, who became the great baptizer and precursor of Jesus.

For the broad dissemination of the youthful Monroe initiative, it was surely important that, from the start, many members of varying congregations and orders participated in the astonishingly successful six-week summer schools of prayer. As far back as 1970, more and more places in North America were the site of six-week summer sessions of the prayer school. These were, first of all, in practically every case, valuable "pre-schools" on the North American continent for the opening of permanent houses and schools of prayer all over the world.

By 1975, Sister Ann Chester could announce that she knew the addresses of seventy or more such permanent houses. She wrote that Kresge House had an enormous volume of correspondence. "Letters come from all over the world, especially when Father Häring is on his travels," she wrote in her book *Prayer Now: A Response to the Needs for Prayer Renewal.*

Sister Chester describes my participation as primarily that of someone who stimulated and encouraged people to trust in the power of the Holy Spirit. Their ears and hearts were penetrated by my invitation to be creative and open.

For my part, I can safely say that in the story of the evolution of the houses-of-prayer movement, I have received more than I gave. One becomes, as it were, a new person, when one receives the gift of living for a long time in an atmosphere of enthusiasm, of mutual trust and praise of God. The meaning of charism becomes uniquely perceptible when so many charisms flow together, as we experienced so intensively at the beginning of the movement.

Father Häring, far left, in front of St. Peter's, Rome, with some of his former students

In Togo, 1973

With Trappist Thomas Merton

Meeting Bishop Fulton J. Sheen, Rome

A book signing, São Paulo, Brazil, 1967

Receiving gift in Tanzania, 1966

Garden at the Academia Alphonsiana, Rome

In Indonesia

Father Häring, right, in Lesotho, South Africa

At airport reception in Warsaw, Poland, 1971

With fellow Redemptorists at their dwelling among the favelas and faveladas in São Paulo, 1987

Father Häring, center, at Gars am Inn, with visitors from Japan, 1995

Father Häring, left, receiving the Wladmierz Pietzak prize in Poland, 1979

Father Häring, left, at the Shrine of Ste. Anne de Beaupre, outside
Quebec City, Canada, 1987

CHAPTER 10

MY LIFE IN THE CHURCH

More and more often one hears from young people, and even from their elders, the phrase, "Jesus—yes, the Church—no!" This phrase reminds us that those who do not get over the crisis in the Church will be badly prepared to deal with the equally widespread crisis in faith. In this chapter, I shall try to communicate to the reader how my experience of the Church turned into an experience of faith.

MY EXPERIENCE OF CHURCH AT HOME

In my parents' house, the healthy wind of the Gospel blew strongly. On long winter evenings, my mother often read to us from the New Testament or from the lives of the great saints. I found my parents and brothers and sisters to be a living Gospel.

My parents were bound in close friendship with the different pastors we had and, above all, with the Franciscan nuns, who ran the local kindergarten and visited and cared for the sick. It was a precious experience of the Church that my parents had such a warm heart for the poor. How amazed I was one morning when we had no bread for breakfast, just potatoes, and mother simply explained, "The mailman is sick, and all his children are going hungry. Are you ready to give up your breakfast bread for them?" Whenever a beggar came around at noontime, how I admired my mother for lovingly saying to him, "Dear guest, today you are invited to lunch with us."

A day never passed without morning and evening prayers, no meal without grace before and afterward. How often I heard the old German rhyme, "*An Gottes Segen / ist alles gelegen*" ("Everything depends on God's blessing"). All in all, our large family struck me as a kind of highly sympathetic Church in miniature. It had, needless to say, an atmosphere of faith, of trust in God, and loving kindness. The family I came from would never have been that way without the Church, which proclaimed the Gospel to us, and without the many men and women who lived out the Gospel in our presence.

The credit for all this has to go primarily to my mother, who gave us a sense of the Church that went far beyond the horizon of our village. We regularly read a magazine about the missions, and on winter nights mother often read us stories about the great missionaries.

It was an experience of Church and of faith when our family, often gathered together in wintertime with visitors from the neighborhood and relatives, recited the rosary and the litany together every night. We absolutely breathed in the hearty air of faith, of faith in God, in Jesus Christ and his Gospel, in the saints. And somehow there on the horizon stood the worldwide Church with its history.

Naturally, we went to Mass every morning. On Sunday we all went to church three times: for solemn Mass in the morning; for vespers in the afternoon; and for the group rosary in the evening. I took it all for granted, again like breathing in and out. In this atmosphere, the question gradually arose of a call to serve the Gospel. On Sunday after Mass, we children all sat in a circle around our father, while mother prepared lunch. Father invited us to say what we had gotten out of the sermon. And it was always moving for me when father himself finally told us what *he* had gotten out of it.

My experience of the Church and faith was what led me to say to my beloved sister Konstantine after I made my first Communion, "I'd like to become saint." And similarly all my childhood experience of the Church came to a head when at long last I plucked up the nerve to tell my mother that I was thinking of becoming a missionary.

My Experience of Church During Years of Study

During my studies, I experienced the Church within me. I could honor and love the Redemptorists, who were my teachers in Gars. Altogether, it was a harmonious and friendship-filled life that I led together with my professors and fellow seminarians. I think back with special gratitude to the religion class taught by Father Baumgartner, who had previously taught dogmatic theology at the house of studies. I found his lectures gripping. You could sense that behind it all was a profound perspective full of joyful faith. And, in the three years at the *Gymnasium* in Günzburg, we were fortunate to have a teacher of religion, Father Gebler, who was humane and greatly gifted both in his field and in his piety. With his extremely sympathetic personality, he stood behind everything that he taught.

As far back as my years in the *Gymnasium*, stormy questions arose in my mind when I read extensively in Church history. It is true that, so far as I can remember, even in my youth I always had a basic tendency to see first and foremost what was good and beautiful about the Church. But then, passionate reader that I was, I ran into the dark century in the history of the papacy—the Inquisition and the use of torture at the behest of the highest church authorities. Granted, this reading hardly caused me to doubt my faith or to feel a temptation to abandon it. But I often complained to the Lord, "Dear God, how could you let all that happen?"

Then, in philosophy and in dogmatic theology, we were fed a diet of Thomism. The Thomistic doctrine of grace maintains that God predetermines everything, or that he denies effective grace in advance, making it metaphysically certain that no good, meritorious acts can take place. When I heard this, I protested, sometimes vehemently, to my learned professors. No other problem bothered—indeed, plagued—me so much as the interaction between Divine Grace (and predestination) and human freedom. Whenever the question arose of the image of God, everything in me got all churned up. It was a consolation, and really helpful for me, to learn that one pope had ordered a truce binding both the Molinists, who viewed everything from the standpoint of human freedom, and the Thomists from the school of Bannez, who saw everything from the angle of God's sovereign predetermination. He insisted that they stop damning one another as heretics, and discuss their dispute in a civilized manner. The solution, in my view, was and is simply to adore the divine mystery.

When the Nazis came to power, I searched avidly for any signs of resistance on the part of the Church. This quest helped me somewhat. Still, as I look back, I often think that I was trying, with help from a certain tendency to repress the harsh truth, to get over the lack of courage on the part of so many representatives of the Church.

My critical potential was in a sense exhausted by my firm rejection of both Communism and Nazism. Today, as I recall those days, I can understand that my position on the

Church was mainly apologetic: I wanted, unconsciously, of course, to make it easier to love the Church. In any case, my love for the Church, even back in my student days, was never blind. I loved the Church as I perceived her to be. But even back then, the failure of some human beings of the Church, including those with high authority, greatly wounded me.

In 1933, when I decided to enter the novitiate and in the following year when I took my first vows, I was under no illusions. I knew that the Church was headed for bad times. Still, I had great confidence in the Church within the total context of an infinitely greater confidence in God. Brave statements by bishops against the Hitler regime were a great encouragement to me. But when it came to contrary reactions by timid bishops, I was blind in one eye. Looking back, I believe that a pronounced inclination to venerate the saints and frequent reading of their biographies did (and still does) help me to maintain a positive attitude toward the Church.

MY EXPERIENCE OF CHURCH IN THE WAR

Amid the unheard of conflict between nations sparked by the insanity and the cruelty of the Second World War, it was extraordinarily comforting to have a continuous, thankful experience of the universality of the Church, or of the Christian world, in France, Poland, the Ukraine, and Russia. People never looked at me as if I were a henchman of the Hitler regime, but as a brother in Christ, the priest glad to serve everyone. In particular, the many proofs of kindness and love from Orthodox Christians in the Ukraine and Russia have done a great deal to shape subsequent parts of my life and prepare me in some ways for service to the ecumene.

When I look back, I am amazed at how many people in the various countries I went to because of the war were spontaneously ready to honor and love the priest as a representative of the Church, even though he was forced to wear a much-hated uniform. For me, all the French men and women, Poles, Ukrainians, and Russians with whom I dealt were sons and daughters of the one heavenly Father and beloved fellow Christians.

MY EXPERIENCE OF CHURCH IN CELEBRATING THE SACRAMENT OF RECONCILIATION

In the course of my long life, I have taken continuous pains to study the history of the sacrament of penance. In the astonishing transformation of the understanding and celebration (or administration) of this sacrament, we see extremely varied forms of how the Church understood many things, including itself. Very early on, I preferred the notion of the sacrament of penance prevailing in the Orthodox Churches. I was deeply impressed when, in Russia or the Ukraine, I saw how priests and penitents stood together in front of an icon, praising God's grace. I myself view the sacrament of reconciliation as a praising confession of sin and a praising proclamation of Messianic peace, as a dispatching of helpers dedicated to the service of peace.

Here in Gars, in many neighboring parishes, at the missions that I repeatedly joined in preaching during the first ten years after the war, in Rome, and in the United States, I was a popular confessor. Once, in Rome, I met with two radio journalists who had already interviewed me a number of times before and were themselves on the point of going back to confession. They questioned me in detail about how I saw this sacrament and how I celebrated it. Before I left the building where I had spoken, I could already sense the reaction. The switchboard operator told me, "One call after another keeps coming in; they are all asking, 'Where does that priest live, the one that spoke just now?'"

During the next few days, the two journalists passed along my address; and in the following months so many people came to St. Alfonso's asking to make their confession with me that I was afraid I would not have any time left over for study. There was no relief until the long summer break. Nonetheless, it was always a great joy for me when I saw people going home from confession relieved, encouraged, and even joyful. When penitents find in the priest an image of the all-merciful Father, of Christ bringing salvation and healing, when they sense something of the breath of love from the Holy Spirit, *that* is a successful experience of the Church—and it also comes flowing back again to the priest.

My Experience of Church As a Giver of Missions

Fifty, even forty, years ago missions were great events for the entire parish. Through my research and writings on the sociology of pastoral care, I helped out with preparations for the two great regional missions in and around Landshut and Ulm; and throughout the entire mission I was active in one of the parishes.

Here I will give only a pair of examples of two very different experiences of the Church. In Kolbermoor, a town south of Munich, I had to fill in for three weeks, at a mission during my Easter vacation. When I returned to the sacristy after my final sermon, the sacristan, a man of about fifty, announced in the presence of my fellow Redemptorists and some priests from the neighborhood, "So, Father Häring, now you have reconciled with the Church all the ones that the last mission drove out fourteen years ago."

On average I spent more than ten hours a day in the confessional. It was like that in a parish in the Landshut area; one after another my penitents would say, "My last confession was thirteen years ago." Finally, I asked one of them, "Wait a minute, thirteen isn't some sort of holy number. How is it that you stopped going to confession exactly thirteen years ago?" The man smiled at me and said, "Are you the only stranger here? Thirteen years ago the missionaries were so superstrict that they all but drove us out of the Church."

One's experience of the Church depends very much upon what image and understanding one has of the Church and wishes to pass on. There is a certain "law of the echo" here.

At the missions for refugees in the Protestant diaspora, one of our main goals, after proclaiming the joyous and consoling message of the Good News, was to call into life viable faith communities. Some years later I came back to the same places; and it was a joy to see how the Church can grow.

My Experience of Church As a Professor of Theology

I was always being asked, whether in Gars, Rome, or by the ecumenical theological faculties in the United States, what sort of understanding of the Church I transmit through my statements and my behavior. I thought it was my urgent task to create friendship. The teacher of theology has to strive to honor Christ as the "Son of man," which, translated clearly and precisely, means "One of us."

I wanted, above all, to be a friend and brother to my students. I think I can say that this determined the atmosphere of my classes. Again and again in dealing with my students and former students, I have experienced the Church as an all-embracing "friendship gathered around Christ."

I have tried to lead my students to love of the Church and, at the same time, to critical thinking. And, to an extent I never dreamed of, they have taught me to communicate theologically. Schools of theology should be an image of the Church as the people of God en route, as a tireless seeker after more light. Looking back, I believe I can say that everywhere and down through the decades I have experienced my life together with my students as a "learning Church." Without asking about how things are usually done, I have begun every lecture with a carefully composed prayer in keeping with the particular goal of the lecture. At the end, I usually said a spontaneous prayer, summarizing what had been learned and felt in the previous hour.

Over all the years, I have gotten more love than I can say from my audiences, and that too counts for me as an experience of Church. And I can look back at quite a long line of students, male and female, who, with grateful pride, can say, "We are the Church." During the semesters I spent at Yale Divinity School and at Union Theological Seminary, evening prayer groups, accompanied by discussions about religion and marked by spontaneous prayer, especially the prayer of praise, came into being with no prompting from me, proving, once again, that prayer can begin to break down many barriers.

MY FIRST EXPERIENCE OF CHURCH IN ROME

I remember my great anticipation at the prospect of seeing a grand papal Mass in St. Peter's. This experience was first given to me under Pius XII. To my amazement, what I saw in the pope was a person who seemed to be the embodiment of dignity, almost of royal majesty. He was carried in on a thronelike chair, surrounded by representatives of the high

Roman nobility in splendid uniforms. A long procession of cardinals marched along with him, each one with a train over thirty-five feet long, and each with two train bearers, most of whom were theology students who were proud to perform such a distinguished service. And there were all sorts of other fancy trimmings. Then I thought about Jesus' entrance into Jerusalem on a wretched donkey. When I wondered out loud in our generalate about such an archaic image of the Church as represented by these trappings and trimmings, a consultor general told me, "In Rome, one's faith is trimmed down—and that does it good."

A few years later, when a number of ceremonial features were simplified, that is, the cardinals' trains were shortened by a quarter, some of the cardinals got upset. The influential Cardinal Nicola Canali came to the burial of Pius XII, along with two of his friends, in old-fashioned splendor and with their traditional full-length trains. The Church, whose image is reflected in the Vatican, evidently has a hard time sloughing off its antiquated and unevangelical legacy. Far more than we wish to admit, we are prisoners of many traditions that no longer have any meaning.

In those days, the gorgeous display of pomp in and around the Vatican still had its admirers, not to mention interested flatterers. What a liberation it was to witness the simplicity and healthy humor of Pope John XXIII.

Looking back, I can say that all the great to-do, all the splendid display, and the many expressions of unevangelical triumphalism sometimes made me sad. But it never tested my faith. I kept thinking: God has enough reasons to laugh at all of us at one time or another. I was more than a little surprised to notice that many of my learned colleagues around the world thought that all this manifold splendor of Vatican ceremonial impressed believers, and so little or none of it should be changed. As always, I wonder: Are not we all, to a great extent, the product of our immediate and not-so-immediate environment?

My Experience of Church Under the Fresh Air of John XXIII

My experience of the Church under Pope John felt liberating; indeed, it was one long sigh of relief. On the day of his election, I was with a Polish colleague on St. Peter's Square, waiting for the results. This particular Polish priest had already come there twice, in vain. Now he was disappointed and wanted to leave. "Stay," I told him, "today you will see the election."

I did not have any special revelation, of course; but I did have a feeling that gradually it had gotten to be time. There were some young Italians standing around us, and they acted very disappointed when the announcement was made. "How can the cardinals choose such an old man?" they said. I got into a conversation with them and made bold to tell these very earnest and appealing men and women, "You will be amazed yet. I believe in surprises."

Very soon there were visible signs that fresh air *was* blowing through the Vatican. But this feeling had nothing to do with the fact that the pope was very well-disposed to me. You could immediately sense his originality. The announcement of an ecumenical council by John XXIII was a sign, a hint, of the great possibilities that lay ahead.

Not much later, I received palpable evidence of his kindness. Though neither he nor I had asked for it, the superior general of my order got a letter in which the pope expressed his recognition, in the warmest terms, for my work *The Law of Christ*. Meanwhile, this same work was under investigation by the Holy Office because letters of complaint that were being sent to that body. I was glad to think and feel that somehow this kindly pope and I were on the same wavelength.

Shortly after the election of Pope John XXIII, I took the train to Bologna at the invitation of Cardinal Giacomo Lercaro. In the same compartment with me sat a little group of pious Roman women. They were saying how alarmed they were that after the ascetical Pius XII, who so thoroughly radiated dignity, a fat, folksy man like John XXIII had ascended the throne of St. Peter.

There was and still is today a minority among the clergy, and no doubt among the laity as well, that could not make its peace with the character and thought of John XXIII. Here is but one example in lieu of many others. Shortly after the death of this humble pope, I met in the hall of the Council a high official from the Roman congregation in charge of canonizations. When I unsuspectingly said to him, "Now you'll have a pleasant job—the beatification and canonization of Pope John," the prelate exploded with indignation. "But where is the saintliness? Where is the virtue of prudence?" I was, of course, taken aback by his comments. But my feelings were these: I had no objections to the beatification of Pius XII, but I consider that the mind of John XXIII—and everything else about him—was closer to the core of the Gospel and the ideal of Petrine service than the overall picture of his immediate predecessor. It is part of the pluralism in our Church that we can come to terms with undeniable differences without harsh rejections or aversions. That is how I experience the Church.

After the election of Pope John Paul I, I felt the same joy as after the election of Pope John XXIII. He, too, was someone I already knew well. He was probably the first Italian professor of moral theology to introduce *The Law of Christ* as a textbook in his course. I especially admired his absolute simplicity and his radiantly joyful face. After his sudden death, I was even sadder than I had been after the death of Pope John. The ways of God ways are unfathomable.

MY EXPERIENCE OF CHURCH UNDER PAUL VI

I had no problems with welcoming the election of Giovanni Battista Montini as Paul VI. He was someone I had long known and esteemed. Pope John, too, had doubtless esteemed him, although in his whole manner Paul VI was anything but a carbon copy of John XXIII. I was quite surprised when, in the first year of his pontificate, Paul VI assigned me the job of preaching the Lenten exercises to him and the Roman Curia. By way of preparation, I reread the book of my patron, Saint Bernard, *De consideratione libri quinque ad Eugenium III*, his spiritual exercises for a pope who was from his own order (the Cistercians) and who was his former student. Then, before quoting one of the most forceful lines from that book, I expressly noted that I could match this saintly preacher neither in holiness nor frankness. Indeed, I felt that the enormous distance between us was positively painful. But Paul VI whispered in my ear, "Have no fear, speak frankly!"

I was much taken with the seriousness and piety of all the participants. Still, the sacristan, a monsignor, warned me after the fourth and fifth talk, "If you go on like this, the pope will grab you by the ears." But that never happened. At the end of the six-day retreat, in about ten minutes, the pope gave a wonderful summary of my basic ideas and concerns. The core of it all, he said, was *paraklesis*, encouragement in the power of the Holy Spirit. On the next day, *L'Osservatore Romano* told its readers that, in memory of these exercises, the pope had ordered that from now on, the phrase "Praised be the Holy Spirit, the Paraclete," was to be added to the litany of praise.

MY EXPERIENCE OF CHURCH
AT THE SECOND VATICAN COUNCIL

In an earlier chapter, I spoke of my participation in the work of the Second Vatican Council. But here I would like to speak briefly about that time as a high point of my experience of faith. The mere announcement by John XXIII that the Council would be held was for me a peak experience of faith expressive of the help of the Spirit of God in and for the Church. The Spirit can surprise and stir us up in marvelous ways. From the inauguration of the Council to its conclusion, the key to my experience of the Church was to see her as a "holy penitent," with a constant need and readiness for renewal, as a Church that thinks and behaves like the wandering people of God.

During the preparatory time, I sometimes felt a strong tension between the vanguard and the stragglers or brakemen who held up the rear. Shortly before the end of the Council, Cardinal Pietro Parente said to me in a threatening tone, "Now we have got to slam on the brakes." Whereupon I felt free to ask, "But haven't you always been a specialist in braking?"

As the Council went on, there were more than a few scattered "fits of courage." We experienced—sometimes more, sometimes less—a Church that dared to launch out on the high seas, a Church that was discovering new horizons and setting out with full trust in God. We experienced a Church that was transforming and renewing itself from a Latin Church to one that was becoming the "salt of the earth," a Church that was discovering new dimensions of its catholicity, a Church bravely preparing itself for its ecumenical vocation.

The Council gave me a whole new perspective on the tenet from the Creed, "I believe in the Holy Spirit, the Lord and Giver of Life." Both during and after the Council, we also experienced storms over the Church. And some people, whether on Peter's side or not, cried out in terror when they thought they were sinking, "Lord, save me" (Mt 14:30). To my mind, the men and women in the vanguard did not always summon up the necessary patience and power of attraction so as to draw along, if possible, the whole of the rear guard. I, too, sometimes found myself lacking patience toward one group or another.

Still, the experience of the Second Vatican Council as a departure for new shores etched itself deeply into my soul. This vision helps me whenever I revive and gratefully recall the best of my previous experiences with the Church, especially in view of other, less encouraging interactions.

MY EXPERIENCE OF CHURCH IN THE THIRD WORLD

The First Vatican Council was thoroughly European and Eurocentric. People still wanted to go on talking exclusively in "Latin" to all Asians, Africans, the ancient nations of the Americas, and so on. If they wanted to enter Peter's bark, people had to use the very narrow gangplank of Roman thinking. Vatican II was the first council with a worldwide representation and an opening—though still a hesitant one, of course—to the multiplicity of cultures. The new sense of catholicity, however, was not yet strong enough to let us break out completely from the armada where one and only one flag was flying. Nevertheless, the dynamic was clear, refreshing, and encouraging.

My many students of the Academia Alfonsiana from Africa, Asia, and Latin America served in many ways as a bridge. A long string of men who had taken my courses at Lumen Vitae (the international catechetical institute in Brussels) showed up at the Council as bishops. I made many new friends among the bishops and theologians from the Third World. During and after the Council, I became part of a mighty Exodus-experience. Even before I became a globetrotting spokesman on conciliar matters, I had "gotten going" intellectually and spiritually.

These friendships resulted in my receiving invitations from all over the world. From 1965 to 1980 (the year I finally lost my larynx), I studied and helped with the inculturation of the Council into a total of ten Asian countries, seventeen African countries, and the great continent of Latin America.

I summarized my experiences of the Church in Africa in by book entitled *I Have Learned With Open Eyes*. There is only one way that we Europeans can help the utterly different cultures of Africa and Asia, and the mixed populations and ancient cultures of the Americas, to interpret the message of the New Testament.

We must come to them as students, as people ready to learn; and we must not hesitate to admit the mistakes—almost incredible as they now seem today—made in Latinizing alien cultures. The only way we can immunize ourselves against such tendencies is to realize and concede that we are still not free from such impulses toward cultural and ecclesial colonization.

I thank Divine Providence and the countless persons and groups that have helped me to broaden my own perspective and to make a similar learning process palatable to others. We will grasp the opportunity to unlearn and learn anew only to the extent that we admit to ourselves and others how much narrowness and one-sidedness we had—and probably still have—to overcome.

MY EXPERIENCE OF CHURCH IN THE PRACTICE OF PASTORAL CARE

Wherever I taught, I had lots of students coming to me for confession or asking me to accompany them on the path to continual conversion. Then, too, I gave hundreds of retreats and continuing-education courses on theological topics all over the world. I do not have the heart to try to count them up. In hindsight, I am amazed how I could take on so many jobs. Part of the reason is, no doubt, that I always found joy in being of service to the Gospel and to my fellow human beings.

Priests and laypeople came to me, hoping for therapy, healing, and encouragement. At times when I felt that God was using me as an instrument of his healing love, I associated a particular feeling with this type of experience. This feeling was sometimes quite profound. I seemed to have sensed that in people who are suffering psychologically I encounter Jesus himself and that he asks me whether or not I am ready to honor him in the least of his brothers and sisters. I believe that religiously based, deep reverence for broken men and women is a crucial factor in their process of healing and integration.

Sometimes, I found help in thinking about the parable of Noah's ark. This is how I tell it. One day Noah complained bitterly to the owner of his ark: "Why did you pen me up with all these strange animals, with the skunks, with the impudent apes, and all these noisy brats?" The Lord looked lovingly at Noah and whispered in his ear, "Never forget that you, too, are one of these fundamentally lovable animals."

Psychologically tormented and frequently misunderstood people have a keen sense for what is happening when we meet them with a deep reverence, just as if we might be showing such reverence to Jesus himself.

I often had to deal with men and women who were evidently suffering from "ecclesiogenic" neuroses. Someone had dinned into their heads the idea of a small-time chief inspector or an avenging God, a God whose highest priority is to demand that we obey his many laws, down to the tiniest, by threatening punishment. These people were shell-shocked by the experience of an angry father or a furious priest who taught them that through him God was speaking, raging, judging, and punishing.

Our pastoral care, our preaching, our efforts to bring salvation depend not least of all on what image of God is stamped in us and what image of God we radiate, consciously or otherwise. I have met every kind of priest: many splendid and sympathetic men, but also priests who were shattered, misdirected, gasping for breath, and tormented. Fortunately, in my long life and in my various activities, I have again and again met with the former—splendid, psychologically healthy priests who radiated joy and kindness. But the experience of the opposite can also be useful to us in finding our way and helping others.

MY EXPERIENCE OF CHURCH IN SERVICE TO FELLOW PRIESTS

My multilayered experiences as a pastoral caregiver made it increasingly clear how important it is in general, but most especially for the training of priests, that our understanding of the Church and our image of human beings be stamped by loving familiarity with Jesus, the nonviolent Savior wholly dedicated to reconciling love—Christ the Healer who reminds us that he has not come to judge, but to heal. For this reason, I have always scrutinized myself, both regarding my work as a teacher of theology and as a pastoral caregiver, to see whether my image of God, my image of the Church, and my image of humanity were in tune.

In my activities in priestly training and in service to them, I am always concerned with the healthy self-image of priests, who through their whole existence and their work credibly reflect the true biblical image of God and a corresponding image of the Church. The question of celibacy was never at the center of my pastoral care for priests or seminarians. But it was by no means marginal either. By way of a preliminary remark which bears on this issue, let me say that I freely chose celibacy, and that when I did, I knew clearly enough what it meant, what crises this choice can be threatened with, and that even good priests can come to grief over celibacy. My approach to complex problems is always existentially influenced. I can make clear distinctions, but I cannot ignore my own attitudes and experience.

On this issue, I have always raised with great urgency the question of how the concrete experience of the law of celibacy plays a part in modeling our image of the Church— indeed the whole of our experience of faith.

Back in the years before the Second Vatican Council, I often had priests come to me who were in a crisis or who had already left the priesthood and gotten married, often in a civil ceremony. This seeking out would often happen in the context of my giving spiritual exercises for priests, of my teaching courses, of my celebrating the sacrament of penance, or as a result of statements I have made in some of my books. The question posed by these priests and by myself was always: what do laws, their implementation and harsh sanctions, have to do with the Church's understanding of itself, with our own image of the Church, and with our experience of faith?

I devoted special attention to this topic in the exercises that I preached for Pope Paul VI and the Curia. I put my reflections under the image of Mary, the mother of mercy. By lovingly focusing on her, we can get a deeper understanding of Jesus' core message: "Be merciful, just as your Father is merciful" (Lk 6:36). Mary corresponds exactly to Jesus' saying in the Gospel, "Be perfect, therefore, as your heavenly Father is perfect" (Mt 5:48). God unmistakably reveals to us in Jesus Christ that his perfection coincides with his mercy.

But then the unavoidable questions arise: Is the Roman Catholic Church's current practice with regard to the law of celibacy merciful as the Father of our Lord Jesus Christ is merciful? Was the Church merciful when for centuries it all but completely barred access to the priesthood for the native population of Latin America? (In accordance with the Roman or colonial Spanish viewpoint that made celibacy the only consideration, it judged them incapable of becoming priests.) Is the Church faithful to the testament of Jesus, who has given us the Eucharist as the bread of life and as a precious legacy, when because of its law of celibacy it prevents, for all practical purposes, the majority of Catholics worldwide from having regular celebrations of the Eucharist?

Yet these questions posed themselves to me much more deeply and more concretely in the face of the difficult encounters I have had with priests who, as the saying goes, have "come to grief over celibacy." Interestingly, in terms of the difficulties facing the priesthood, no one talks about failure when it comes to the proud, hard-hearted, or ambitious priests.

MY EXPERIENCE OF CHURCH
AS A COUNSELOR TO THE CONFLICTED

Until the pontificate of Paul VI, we priests had no authority to absolve someone who had left the priesthood, unless he had practiced complete continence for at least a year. Even then, we could give absolution only with explicit authorization from Rome. Like everyone else, I abided strictly by these regulations. In fact, several married priests had been motivated by me to take this path of yearlong continence. All except one failed to last a full year. In this case, I had stressed to the ex-priest that he should be very loving and tender to his wife; and then they both managed to meet this requirement. I say, "they," because the wife must take this commitment just as seriously as does the man. Normally, these married priests were urgently admonished, for the sake of continence, to remain aloof and not to engage in displays of affection with their wives.

But did that outcome mean I had no way of letting off the others who could neither dismiss the mother of their children nor live in total continence? I suggested another way: strive to be merciful by following the model of Jesus and his heavenly Father. Then you have the Gospel's consoling assurance that the Lord will be infinitely more merciful with you. When I was in Rome, I was occasionally forced—so as not to make such consoling language useless—to come up with ways of helping that sort of priest and his family when they were in dire need. Thus, over the years, I paid the doctor's and druggist's bills for a former monsignor and his children. According to the Concordat of 1929, the Italian state was forbidden to give such "ex-priests" any sort of employment. This rule was clearly part of an unevangelical system of sanctions.

Immediately after my sermon before the pope that dealt

with the stern question of whether, given the previous practice of the Church, we had the right to claim that we venerated the "mother of mercy," I got a note from John XXIII's former secretary, Monsignor Loris Capovilla. In it, he observed that, on his deathbed, Pope John had expressed his great pain over the fact that he had not resolved this issue.

Paul VI spoke at length with me and told me to send him as soon as possible a memorandum about what should be done now. He was not just deeply moved by thoughts of the bitter suffering of the people affected. Like me, he was ultimately concerned with the understanding of the Church, with a view to the experience of faith in the all-merciful Father. After just a short time, the petitions awaiting action were given a favorable answer. The marriages were made canonically valid without any conditions. But many of us, including the pope, were shaken by the very large number of priests who had been still serving their parishes and now submitted requests to be laicized.

So it is more or less understandable that John Paul II wanted to take remedial action instantly by at first denying every single dispensation. And so the whole system of sanctions and harsh measures came back into force again. It took several tries before the Union of Superiors General got the pope to moderate his strategy somewhat.

Tens of thousands of priests have given up their duties and been married in civil ceremonies, without getting a dispensation or even trying to get one. And many no doubt did so with a subjectively good conscience.

For me, *this* experience of the Church, which also applies to the pastoral care of divorced and remarried couples, has been extremely painful. As I see it, behind these occurrences lies a completely different image of God, a different sort of faith-experience, a completely different view of the relationship between charism and law, and between grace and law. It is a relic of the moral theology that was used to hammer in countless minor laws (for example, concerning ritual) under penalty of mortal sin, without asking, as we did, in shock: "What kind of an image of God is this? What kind of image of the Church of Christ?" The Church—all of us—has to reappraise our past in a joint passionate effort to get to know Jesus and his Gospel better.

The bishops were heard to say that these questions above were not the core questions of faith, that nowadays what was at stake was the question of God. My answer is that the question of God in the abstract doesn't exist. We believe in the God of history, the creator of the world and the human race. Isn't it obvious that behind all the requests of concerned laypeople stands an image of God in harmony with the Gospel's image of God, and a pastoral care alert to the signs of the time?

Now that the ordination of married men (*viri probati*) as permanent deacons, which had been demanded on all sides, has come to pass, then perhaps we will also see the reintegration into full service of those priests who, apart from celibacy, are credible pastoral caregivers. I personally know many of them who, despite everything, are truly devoted to the Church and whose apostolic work has been rich in blessings.

MY EXPERIENCE OF AN INQUISITOR CHURCH

Here I refer to my years of conflict with Vatican authorities, especially with the Congregation for the Doctrine of the Faith. This authority is the legal successor to the Holy Office on the Inquisition, and, in my earlier days, was known as *Suprema Sancta Congregatio Sancti Offici,* or Supreme Sacred Congregation of the Holy Office.

The roughness of my hearings before this august body can be indicated by one, brief incident. After a second and then a third questioner had bellowed at me, I made bold to say, "Gentlemen, let us not forget the whole prior history of this organization." To my astonishment, Archbishop Jean Jerome Hamer, the secretary of the congregation, replied, "We are proud of that history of ours." Was this a sign of institutional incapacity for repentance or was it simply a lack of historical education on the part of this man (whose nomination to the cardinalate was by that time as good as certain)? Was it a conscious yes to the method and structures of the Inquisition? Or was it both—or a rare mixture of several levels? In any case, when I heard this remark, a chill went through my bones.

It is reported, when the fire for burning Savonarola at the stake had already been lit, the Inquisitor pronounced the usual formula: *"Abscindo te ab ecclesia miltante, abscindo te ab ecclesia triumphante,"* ("I cut you off from the Church Militant, I cut you off from the Church Triumphant"). The Church as embodied in the Inquisition was both militant and triumphalistic, but the Inquisitor thought of the heavenly Church as the absolutely direct continuation of the earthly Church of his day. Savonarola, known as the Florentine prophet, is said to have replied, "You can cut me off from this all too militant Church. Fortunately, you have no authority over the heavenly Church."

No doubt it has to be granted that, for all its apparent historical continuity, the institution that I had to deal with then was incomparably more humane than its predecessor. They didn't want to do me any bodily harm—not deliberately at least.

Back then and on other occasions as well, I was ordered to promise, orally and in writing, to avoid not just every explicit dissent from Vatican teachings, but every appearance of dissent as well. Then I would be allowed to live in the Church in peace and honor. For myself, however, this meant dishonoring the Church through insincerity, and polluting my personal and ecclesial conscience and consciousness. That is what I would be doing were I to sign myself over to conformism with this historically conditioned organization; and this blind conformance was what they were demanding from me.

MY EXPERIENCE OF CHURCH AT DOCTRINAL EXAMINATIONS

The two endlessly long official indictments, which, according to Archbishop Hamer, came from "two great moralists," were crawling with incredible misrepresentations. The basis for the accusations was my book, published in Italian and translated from the original German whose title in English is *Healing Service: Ethical Problems of Modern Medicine* (1971). The only text my accusers looked at was the Italian translation, while the German and English editions, which I had written myself, were totally ignored. The book was widely praised by my colleagues in the field and raised no serious objections. Thousands of physicians prized the book.

The doctrinal proceedings also had an effect on my health. For their part, the men responsible for that "trial" surely weren't worried about this. They scarcely understood (and still don't understand) that one's suffering under such circumstances is in direct proportion to one's love for the Church. During the years that the hearings dragged on, I came down with throat cancer. Wasn't this a kind of response by my body to the fact that the congregation was "going for the jugular"?

Since the topic under investigation was in the area of medical ethics, scholarly experts in this field must have had some worrisome thoughts both in advance of and during the proceedings. I wonder whether thoughts like that had ever occurred to anyone of the "Sacred Inquisition" in the course of the history of the Church?

A much weightier consideration for me was the fact that the "trial" was continued or set in motion again, after I already had three operations for cancer behind me and even though I had expressly brought up the issue of my health with the Congregation. Surely there was some connection between the drawn-out hearings and the way the cancer kept coming back, so that for years I had to fight for my life. In the end, I lost not just my larynx but the upper section of my windpipe. Needless to say, the authorities had no conscious intention of provoking any of this, as if they had literally wanted to silence me. But was it not just another sign of how they live in a completely different world from us ordinary mortals? Is it not a case of incompetent competence?

I am not going back over this out of resentment. If I hadn't forgiven these individuals from the heart, my feelings of resentment would most likely have helped to strengthen the cancer and make it more than my inner resources could bear.

What I am concerned with here is, as always, the image of the Church, the Church's understanding of itself. I see the image of the Church in its great and many little saints, in its outspoken prophets. The procedure and behavior of the Congregation did not tempt me to deny my faith, simply because I never identified this organization with the Church as a whole, with the Church as such.

Nevertheless, since it is an important authoritative body in the Church, all those who have any share of responsibility for it have to radically ask themselves: *What sort of understanding of the Church, what image of the Church and even of God is at issue here?* By quite consciously putting it in this way, I protected myself against the shipwreck of my faith in God, my faith in the Gospel, and my faith in the Church as a whole.

After the publication of my book called in English *My Witness for the Church,* which was translated into many languages, I received more than a thousand letters from readers of the book. Some of these letters were very moving, as correspondents told me of many examples of its influence. They would write, "Thanks to this book I have decided not to leave the Church," "Our grown-up sons have decided to return to the Church," and other such similar messages.

Around fifty letters contained some friendly chiding. Some other letters could be explained only by assuming that their writers were mentally ill. I sent amicable answers to everyone who reproached me, whether politely or not. In most cases, I received an equally friendly response.

Someone sent me an issue of the American magazine *The Wanderer,* with a long letter from a reader who happened to be an old priest. In it, the man intoned a hymn of praise because God had finally punished that old heretic Bernard Häring by taking away, if not his life, at least his voice. I read this "letter" and similar ones with a deep sense of sympathy for the sick people who wrote them.

It was a similar scene when, like many other theologians, I signed the so-called "Cologne Declaration Against Resignation in the Church." Let me point out to readers who may have missed it that this declaration was based on some serious experiences, especially the Congress of Moralists in Rome where Monsignor Carlo Caffarra, the pope's adviser, equated artificial birth control with murder. As for myself and most of my colleagues, we were not really concerned with protest as such, but primarily with contributing to the formation of people's consciences and preventing a mass exodus from the Church.

MY EXPERIENCE OF A CHURCH FACED WITH LOVING CRITICISM

We see clearly from the Gospels that the love of Jesus for his apostles and disciples was often a critical love. We have to examine our own conscience as well with a view to Jesus' critical love for us. The Church is rightly very critical when it comes to beatifying or canonizing someone. And we all have to learn from Jesus how to love our Church (which includes ourselves) critically. The word *criticism* comes from the Greek root *krinein*, "to judge or distinguish." Concretely speaking, when we call the Church holy, we are looking at the saints, not at muddled human beings. For example, we don't take Pope Alexander VI as an example of chastity. In our pluralistic era, Catholics who blindly conform to everything that comes from Rome are certainly not playing their role as the "salt of the earth."

When I say that our love for the Church has to be critical, that by no means implies approval or recommendation of loveless or constantly negative criticism. Only those who have clear-eyed vision and praise for what is good in the Church can offer healthy criticism about what is and is not in unison with the Gospel and with the signs of the times, correctly understood.

For me and my generation, it was a long trek from the rather uncritical thinking in a closed peasant village and in a closed society to a fully developed "virtue of loving criticism." Our models are the great prophets of Israel and the great prophetic figures of the Christian world. Only a critical love that strives throughout all of life for the gift of the discernment of spirits can effectively unmask the Satanic temptations to which we—and the Church as an institution in its officeholders—are exposed.

In my view, the Second Vatican Council was one of the greatest experiences of the virtue of criticism: a grand effort in solidarity to exercise the gift of discernment, to see what holds promise for the future in the life of the Church, to foster it and to get rid of useless routine.

Let me come back just one more time to the key goal of the doctrinal hearings against me: I was told to make an oral and written commitment to avoid not just all dissent, but every word that might be taken for dissent. This was likewise the point of introducing a special loyalty oath required for theologians, bishops, and everyone who directly serves the Church. The oath called for the uncritical acceptance and advocacy of all the pope's teachings, and it was supposed to stand right alongside the Creed. One can imagine what would happen with the whole theological enterprise if we all agreed to take such an oath. It would also do no good for unity in the faith, because faith comes from the heart, from a convinced conscience. The result would be an immovable and often insincere conformism. Again, we need only imagine what would have happened if Friedrich von Spee, the great seventeenth-century Jesuit, had bound himself by oath to say nothing against the Church's theory and practice of torture and witch trials in his day.

Human beings who have been permanently sterilized or castrated can no longer transmit life. Much the same is true of theologians who are sworn to conformism. To tell them, "Be creative!" would have to be taken as some kind of sarcasm. And it would be a pure illusion to expect them to be able to serve ecumenical dialogue and the credibility of the Gospel in a critical age, or to keep an eye on the signs of the times so as to free the core of faith from all its historical excrescences. Without absolute honesty and sincerity in theological thought, there can be no credibility. And without a healthy pluralism in the theology of the worldwide Church, there can be no inculturation of all peoples and cultures. It was only because of this concern that I decided to speak openly about my unpleasant experiences with the Roman Congregation of the Faith.

CHAPTER 11

IN RETIREMENT

For my sixty-fifth birthday, my colleagues and Redemptorist brethren, along with friends and former students, put together a *festschrift* that turned out very well. But it was ultimately an open question as to whether I would be alive to celebrate that birthday. A few weeks earlier, I had had my third operation for cancer—an operation which lasted a good five hours. Day and night I had to remain seated, holding my head in a certain position so that the unusually bold and skillful surgery would work. An outstanding ear, nose, and throat specialist had learned in the United States the art of replacing the vocal chords of a cancerous larynx with new vocal chords from the mucous membrane. Patients who underwent this operation must be nonsmokers. I was the first candidate for this surgery my doctor had found in Italy whose mucous membranes had not been ruined by smoke.

When I got up for the first time post-operatively to go to the bathroom, I had a severe cardiac infarction. It was so violent and painful that there was no room for doubt about the seriousness of the situation. I lifted myself up into the bed and waited for the Great Moment, which seemed to be palpably close.

When my current doctor read the results of the first cardiogram, taken almost fourteen years after this attack, the computer yielded the following information: "Situation after severe cardiac infarction." My doctor asked me, "How did they treat your cardiac infarction?" When I answered, "I didn't even mention it to the doctor, since I was so sure I was going to die; and I didn't want any hustle and bustle around my bed," my doctor's reaction was, "That probably saved your life."

The doctors in Colleferro (south of Rome) soon noticed that I was in an extreme crisis and informed my superiors that Father Häring was on his deathbed. But things worked out otherwise: I recovered very quickly. With the new vocal cords I could speak almost as well as before. So I took up my full schedule again.

But less than three years later, the new vocal cords were eaten away by malign growths (cancer). After unsuccessful partial operations, they sent me back to Germany in hopes of finding a doctor who would once again venture to do the extremely complicated surgery. Around the beginning of February, Professor Westhues in Starnberg operated on me. Meanwhile I had gone on a forty-two day fast, eating nothing but beetroot juice and unsweetened nettle tea, which totally cleaned out my liver and kidneys. The fast also completely cured me of an old kidney and liver illness that I had contracted in Russia during the war; and so they could risk doing the six-hour operation. Professor Westhues explained, "If there is positively no prospect of success, I won't operate. But if there's even a slight chance, I'll risk it." It worked. I learned relatively quickly to use my esophagus to talk, and once again resumed my full schedule in Rome at the Academia Alfonsiana.

BECOMING A PROFESSOR EMERITUS

After my seventieth birthday, I had a little celebration upon becoming a professor emeritus. At that point, the director of the Academy asked me, "May we look forward to your continuing your activity here for some time longer?" In 1983, I still had quite a number of doctoral candidates to supervise; but the doctor found out that my lungs had expanded by one-third and were thoroughly taken over by cancerous nodules of the same kind that I had had with the throat cancer. He concealed nothing from me, and just prescribed some pills that he thought might slow the cancer down. About five weeks later I told him that I felt better, so he referred me to the best cancer specialist in Rome. After another thorough examination, this man told me: "The lungs have gone back to their normal size; they are no longer pressing against the heart. You can still see the cancer nodules, but they are completely disintegrating." At first I was speechless, then I asked him to explain his findings to me, because I was only too glad to believe him. The famous man tried to find the right words. Finally, he took a picture of Jesus out of his cabinet, pointed at it, and said, "I believe in him."

In 1986, when I was about to leave Rome for good, I was visited by my doctor, who had referred me to the famous specialist. In the presence of his wife, he asked me, "What saints did you pray to? Your sudden cure was most certainly a miracle." The only answer I could give was, "I didn't pray to anyone; at that point, a cure was unthinkable." And that was in fact why I had not prayed. Perhaps my students who still wanted to do their doctorates with me stormed heaven on my behalf.

One last joyful experience in Rome was the beatification of our Redemptorist brother, Kaspar Stanggassinger, who had died in Gars and whom I had revered from my youth. Then it was off to my old/new home in Gars. We have here, I think, an enjoyable community of about twenty-two priests and as many brothers, with a varied round of activities.

My chief responsibility was now simply to learn to live in retirement in a meaningful way. I no longer have any jobs with deadlines or fixed obligations to perform any services. Retirement is a great gift and a lovely responsibility. Now that I am retired I feel like a horse put out to pasture, free from every harness.

THE RICHES OF RETIREMENT

I soon discovered that here in complete repose I can do all sorts of useful and enriching things. First of all, there is my modest collaboration in our continuing-education institute for teachers, at which every year about twelve hundred men and women religion teachers chose one of the many offerings. For some courses that I found particularly interesting, I would sign on to the program at the request of the program's leaders. Much more frequently, a given class would ask, through their teacher, for me to give a talk and spend some time in dialogue. In most cases, I was glad to say yes. Spending a brief hour or two that way did not interfere with my retirement, but only enriched it. This occasional lecturing was also a way to stay in touch with the "joys and hopes, the distress and fears" of our most open-minded contemporaries.

These lively dialogues and the topics we discussed led me to compose several of my briefer works. Thus, for example, after the harsh response by the Vatican to the proposal by three German bishops concerning pastoral care for divorced Catholics, the religion teachers asked me to give my opinion and prognosis for the future. I replied with a talk entitled, "The Future Emerges." When they asked to be allowed to photocopy my text, I agreed. Soon it was making the rounds, and one day the editor of *Stimmen der Zeit* suggested printing it. That was more or less how many of my smaller publications got into print. The echoes prompted by this text led to new reflections and dialogues, and finally to the book *Meine Hoffnung für die Kirche* (in English, *My Hopes for the Church*), published in German by Herder in 1997.

The same thing happened with my lecture, "More Ways Than One," for the catechetical teachers at our summer programs in Gars. Given the lively response it evoked, I broadened and deepened the text, which led to the publication of a book with the same title, a book that was much read and discussed in the German-speaking world and, through translations, beyond it.

It is a special gift of retirement that one can provide people who need advice and consolation with the sure feeling that one has not just an open heart and open ears, but the *time* to listen to them. Among those seeking advice were (and still are) divorced Catholics who have either remarried or who are thinking of it. And so, people came to me, some of them from far away, all quite sincerely trying to find the will of God and hoping to grasp the meaning of this will in their current situation. Out of these conversations and the sympathy I felt for the people involved grew my book whose title in English is *No Way Out? Pastoral Care of the Divorced and Remarried* (1990). The book went through a number of editions in several languages, and I often received grateful letters from readers who felt they had been understood. They noted that the book provided not abstract and unworldy theory, but sympathy inspired by the Gospel.

Of course, one can offer this sort of help only if one

constantly stays *au courant*. That job has been made much easier by the excellent library we have here in Gars.

These years also saw the publication in several languages of my book *"I Have Seen Your Tears": Notes of Support From a Fellow Sufferer,* which likewise grew out of the practice of consoling people. When I tell someone (with my esophagus voice) who is in need of consolation one of my favorite principles, "As redeemed persons, we can still laugh and be joyful," he or she will never think, "That's easy for *him* to say." I am, after all, one of them.

Since the Second Vatican Council, I have had a lively interest in new spiritual movements, above all, the charismatic renewal movement, the Focolare movement (also known as the Work of Mary), and, not least of all, cursillos. In retirement I had, and still have, enough time to write a brief article on the virtues of the Christian adult almost every month for the cursillo magazine *The Gospel Today.* This was done at the request of its editor, Josef Cascales. This long collaboration led to my book *The Virtues of an Authentic Life: A Celebration of Spiritual Maturity.*

GIVING PRIORITY TO REFLECTION AND PRAYER

Retirement also allows me, far more than did my years of hectic activity, to give priority to reflection and prayer. Now I have plenty of time for regular reading of Scripture. I particularly like meditating on Jesus' understanding of himself as the nonviolent Servant of God who is prepared to suffer in fulfillment of the grand prophecies of Second Isaiah. I use every opportunity to preach his healing and liberating love that puts an end to enmity, and to understand our baptismal calling in this light. With increasing age, retirement points me forward ever more clearly in joyful expectation of the eternal, absolutely satisfying state of the final retirement, in which all life will find its blessed fulfillment.

Looking back, I can well say that in the course of my long life, I have experienced no more than my normal share of sickness and pain, and in the process I have been granted, in a quite special and overabundant fashion, the grace and experience of the love of God and my fellow men and women. And so, to the extent that I cultivate a grateful memory, that spirit of praise increases, and I find with ever greater clarity how richly God has blessed me and my life, not least of all through the gift of my present retirement.

In my advanced age, my eyes still glow almost as much as in my younger years. My hearing, it is true, has noticeably declined, but it is still perfectly good enough for a fruitful dialogue, even without a hearing aid.

I think back gratefully on all the help and love I have gotten from competent and loving doctors and members of the nursing profession over the course of my long life. What good fortune for me that precisely during these years I found such a knowledgeable and concerned physician as Dr. Rudolf Englert. To all these people I also largely owe the fact that so far my retirement and old age have not meant any loss of quality of life.

One of the richest sources of strength in retirement is the continually fresh experience of good will, understanding, and friendship. And why can't retirement be just the time for increasing our capacity for sympathizing with others and bringing them joy?

Once we succeed in ridding ourselves, once and for all, of one of our worst primordial enemies, the continuous "ifs, ands, ors, and buts," so that we have fully made room for the joyous "Yes, Father!" then we can go forth to meet the final "Yes, Father!" with ever growing joy.

One of the most precious qualities of retirement is the fact that it can let us understand and shape it completely as a state of expectation. Without the supposition that we desire an escape from the "here and now," we can concentrate instead on giving a full yes to this last, fruitful phase of our life. If we do this, we open ourselves progressively to the "coming things," in happy expectation of the blessed, absolutely fulfilled retirement of the eternal feast of love and joy.

If we wish to look forward to the last transformation, we have to find a clear answer to the question, "What will my death be?" I am not afraid of death as a breaking off; I greet it even now as a breakthrough, a departure to new shores, with growing curiosity, in joyful expectation.

I contemplate and long for my death as the last, irrevocable, and unsurpassable yes and *Amen* to God's salvific will. In gratitude for all the rich harvest experiences during my life, I am glad to look for the decisive harvest day, for death, the going home to the "festive gathering," to community with all the loving souls, all the blessed.

Meanwhile we do not stand alone in mere concern for ourselves. There is more at stake here than merely waiting for the harvest day of our own life; rather we look forward to the common harvest festival of joy, of praise and of happiness with one another.

As long as I live here in the dwelling of my mortal body, I feel that I am not yet wholly and truly in retirement, but in an expectant preretirement, which will not have reached its goal until I rest in the heart of God.

APPENDIX

Brief Chronology of Bernard Häring's Life

November 10, 1912	Birth in Böttingen, Germany
May 1933	Entry into the Redemptorist Novitiate
May 1939	Ordained a priest
1941	Priest-medic in German army stationed in France
1941	Army service in Poland
1941	Stationed on the Russian front
1941	Wounded in battle
1947	Receives Doctorate of Theology degree and resumes teaching at the Redemptorist College at Gars
1950–1953	Part-time professorship at the Academia Alphonsiana, Rome
1954	Publication of *The Law of Christ*
1954–1986	On the faculty of the Academia Alphonsiana, Rome
1962–1965	Participates in the Second Vatican Council
1977–1981	Investigated by the Congregation for the Doctrine of Faith
1978–1981	Publication of *Free and Faithful in Christ*
1986	Retirement at Gars am Inn

APPENDIX

OTHER WORKS BY BERNARD HÄRING

Acting on the Word: Monasticism and Religious Life. New York: Farrar, Straus, 1968.

Bernard Haring Replies: Answers to 50 Moral and Religious Questions. Staten Island, NY: Alba House, 1967.

Blessed Are the Pure in Heart: The Beatitudes. New York: Seabury Press, 1977.

Celebrating Joy. New York: Herder and Herder, 1970.

The Christian Existentialist: the Philosophy and Theology of Self-fulfillment in Modern Society. New York: New York University, 1968.

Christian Maturity. New York: Herder and Herder. 1967.

Christian Renewal in a Changing World. New York: Desclee Co., 1964.

The Church on the Move. Staten Island, New York: Alba House, 1970.

Dare to Be Christian: Developing A Social Conscience. Liguori, MO: Liguori Publications, 1983.

Discovering God's Mercy: Confession Helps for Today's Catholic. Liguori, MO: Liguori Publications, 1980.

Embattled Witness: Memories of a Time of War. New York: Seabury Press, 1976.

Ethics of Manipulation: Issues in Medicine, Behavior Control, and Genetics. New York: Seabury Press, 1976.

The Eucharist and Our Everyday Life. New York: Seabury Press, 1979.

Eucharistic Devotion. Liguori, MO: Liguori Publications, 1987.

Evangelization Today. New York: Notre Dame, IN: Fides Publishers, 1974.

Faith and Morality in the Secular Age. New York: Doubleday, 1973.

Free and Faithful in Christ: Moral Theology for Priests and Laity, Volume 1: General Moral Theology. New York: Seabury, 1978.

Free and Faithful in Christ: Moral Theology for Priests and Laity, Volume 2: The Truth Will Set You Free. New York: Seabury Press, 1979.

Free and Faithful in Christ: Moral Theology for Priests and Laity, Volume 3: Light to the World. New York: Crossroad, 1981.

God's Word and Man's Response. Mahwah, NJ: Paulist Press, 1963.

Heart of Jesus: Symbol of Redeeming Love. Liguori, MO: Liguori Publications, 1983.

Hope Is the Remedy. New York: Doubleday, 1972.

"I Have Seen Your Tears": Notes of Support From a Fellow Sufferer. Liguori, MO: Liguori Publications, 1995.

In Pursuit of Holiness. Liguori, MO: Liguori Publications, 1982.

APPENDIX

In Pursuit of Wholeness: Healing in Today's Church. Liguori, MO: Liguori Publications, 1985.

The Johnnine Council: Witness to Unity. New York: Herder and Herder, 1963.

The Law of Christ: Moral Theology for Priests and Laity, Volume 1: General Moral Theology. Westminster, MD: Newman Press, 1961.

The Law of Christ: Moral Theology for Priests and Laity, Volume 2: Life in Fellowship with God and Man. Westminster, MD: Newman Press, 1963.

The Law of Christ: Moral Theology for Priests and Laity, Volume 3: Man's Assent to the All-Embracing Majesty of God's Love. Westminster, MD: Newman Press, 1966.

The Liberty of the Children of God. Staten Island, NY: Alba House, 1966.

Love Is the Answer. Denville, NJ: Dimension Books, 1970.

Marriage in the Modern World. Westminster, MD: Newman Press, 1965.

Married Love: A Modern Christian View of Marriage and Family Life. Chicago: Argus Books (Peacock Books), 1970.

Mary and Your Everyday Life: A Book of Meditations. Liguori, MO: Liguori Publications, 1978.

Medical Ethics. Notre Dame, IN: Fides Publishers, 1973.

Morality Is for Persons. New York: Farrar, Straus, 1971.

My Witness for the Church. Mahwah, NJ: Paulist Press, 1992.

New Horizons for the Church. Notre Dame, IN: Ave Maria, 1968.

No Way Out. Pastoral Care of the Divorced and Remarried. Slough, England: St. Paul Publications, 1989.

Prayer: the Integration of Faith and Life. Notre Dame, IN: Fides Publishers, 1975.

Priesthood Imperiled: A Critical Examination of Ministry in the Catholic Church. Liguori, MO: Liguori/Triumph, 1996.

Road to Relevance: Present and Future Trends in Catholic Moral Teaching. Staten Island, NY: Alba House, 1970

Road to Renewal: Perspectives of Vatican II. New York: Doubleday, 1968.

Sacramental Spirituality. New York: Sheed & Ward, 1965.

Sacraments in a Secular Age: A Vision in Depth on Sacramentality and Its Impact on Moral Life. Slough, England: St. Pauls Publications, 1976.

The Sacraments and Your Everyday Life. Liguori, MO: Liguori Publications, 1976.

Shalom: Peace, the Sacrament of Reconciliation. New York: Farrar, Straus, 1967.

Sin in the Secular Age. New York: Doubleday, 1974.

This Time of Salvation. New York: Herder and Herder, 1966.

Tolerance: Towards an Ethic of Solidarity and Peace. Staten Island, NY: Alba House, 1995.

APPENDIX

A Theology of Protest. New York: Farrar Straus, 1970.

Toward A Christian Moral Theology. Volume II in Studies and Research in Christian Theology at Notre Dame. Notre Dame, IN: University or Notre Dame Press, 1966.

The Virtues of an Authentic Life: A Celebration of Spiritual Maturity. Liguori, MO: Liguori Publications, 1997.

What Does Christ Want? Staten Island, NY: Alba House, 1968.

INDEX

INDEX

INDEX

INDEX